IT'S GREAT TO BE A MISSIONARY

OTHER BOOKS AND AUDIO BOOKS
BY ED J. PINEGAR

Press Forward Saints

Living by the Word

Your Patriarchal Blessing

Happily Ever After

Power Tools for Missionaries, Four Volumes

After Your Mission

Lengthen Your Shuffle

Series of Latter-Day Commentaries, Teachings and Commentaries, Unlocking, and Who's Who—Old Testament, New Testament, Book of Mormon, and Doctrine and Covenants

The Temple: Gaining Knowledge and Power in the House of the Lord

The Christmas Code

The Christmas List

Preparing for the Melchizedek Priesthood and My Mission

The Little Book of Gratitude

31 Days to a Better You

Fatherhood: A Calling of Love

Ed J. Pinegar

IT'S GREAT TO BE A MISSIONARY

Daily Insights and Inspirations

Covenant Communications, Inc.

Cover image *Gold Field in Sunset* © Mycola, iStockphotography.com
Cover Designed by Christina Marcano

Published by Covenant Communications, Inc.
American Fork, Utah

Printed in the United States of America
First Printing: June 2017

24 23 22 21 20 19 18 17 10 9 8 7 6 5 4 3 2 1

ISBN-13: 978-1-52440-327-0

Introduction

This little book is designed to help and encourage you as you serve your mission. There will be tried-and-true principles you can understand and put into practice. There are inspiring scriptures that will tell you the things you should do. There are stimulating quotes from the prophets and General Authorities to edify and uplift you. Seek to apply these teachings, and they will assist you in your missionary work. There will be material for companionship study and district meetings.

This is a great work—to bring souls unto Christ. Souls are precious. The Prophet Joseph has declared: "After all that has been said, the greatest and most important duty is to preach the Gospel" (Joseph Smith, in *History of the Church*, 2:478). This work is Heavenly Father's and our Savior's work. We have been called to assist Them in this lifesaving and life-exalting work.

You will come to understand the need to do everything by the power of the Holy Spirit. You will come to see the need to obtain the knowledge of the word of God before you can preach the word of God. You will realize the great need for and power of humility, faith, love, and obedience. Everything in missionary work has to do with being directed by the Holy Ghost and inviting people to come unto Christ and being converted to Him.

So you need to be at your best, even like unto the sons of Mosiah:

> Now these sons of Mosiah were with Alma at the time the angel first appeared unto him; therefore Alma did rejoice exceedingly to see his brethren; and what added more to his joy, *they were still his brethren in the Lord*; yea, and *they had waxed strong in the knowledge of the truth; for they were men of a sound understanding and they had searched the scriptures diligently, that they might know the word of God.*
>
> But this is not all; they *had given themselves to much prayer,*

> *and fasting; therefore they had the spirit of prophecy, and the spirit of revelation, and when they taught, they taught with power and authority of God.* (Alma 17:2–3; italics added)

Isn't that amazing!

You have been entrusted like no other generation to go forth at a younger age. Much is expected of you. And the great news is that you can do it. You have been prepared. You have been called. So go forth, for now is the time. You are the ones. And the place? Wherever you serve your Heavenly Father's children. They are waiting for you to bring them to Christ. This is your glory and joy.

O Ye That Embark in the Service of God

Now behold, a marvelous work is about to come forth among the children of men.

Therefore, O ye that embark in the service of God, see that ye serve him with all your heart, might, mind and strength, that ye may stand blameless before God at the last day.

Therefore, if ye have desires to serve God ye are called to the work;

For behold the field is white already to harvest; and lo, he that thrusteth in his sickle with his might, the same layeth up in store that he perisheth not, but bringeth salvation to his soul;

And faith, hope, charity and love, with an eye single to the glory of God, qualify him for the work.

Remember faith, virtue, knowledge, temperance, patience, brotherly kindness, godliness, charity, humility, diligence.

Ask, and ye shall receive; knock, and it shall be opened unto you. Amen. (D&C 4:1–7)

Be Anxiously Engaged in the Work

Missionaries should be anxiously engaged in work. My brethren, I wonder if we are doing all we can. Are we complacent in our approach to teaching all the world? We have been proselyting now 144 years. Are we prepared to lengthen our stride? To enlarge our vision?

The missionary has a tremendous responsibility, having covenanted to teach the nations. Less than full Church service time can hardly clean the blood from casual hands. Less than a great dedication will hardly free the missionary from blame.

Therefore, it is expedient that missionaries go to with all their hearts, minds, mights, and strengths to meet as many of the proper people under the proper circumstances as possible and bring them to a knowledge of the truth. Constant effort should be made to reduce the fringe items of activity and press into consecrated fruitful hours that time saved from the less essential things. (Spencer W. Kimball, *The Teachings of Spencer W. Kimball*, ed. Edward L. Kimball [1982], 574–75)

Proclaim the Gospel

1) "Go ye therefore, and teach all nations, baptizing them in the name of the Father, and of the Son, and of the Holy Ghost." (Matthew 28:19)

2) "Go ye into all the world, and preach the gospel to every creature" (Mark 16:15). "That repentance and remission of sins should be preached . . . among all nations, beginning at Jerusalem." (Luke 24:47)

3) "For behold, thus said Jesus Christ, the Son of God, unto his disciples who should tarry, yea, and also to all his disciples, in the hearing of the multitude: Go ye into all the world, and preach the gospel to every creature." (Mormon 9:22)

4) "For verily the voice of the Lord is unto all men. . . . And the voice of warning shall be unto all people, by the mouths of my disciples, whom I have chosen in these last days." (D&C 1:2, 4)

Prophets Have Admonished Us to Proclaim the Gospel

After all that has been said, the greatest and most important duty is to preach the Gospel. (Joseph Smith, in *History of the Church*, 2:478)

Our mission has principally been to preach the first principles of the gospel, calling upon men everywhere to believe in the Lord God of heaven, he that created the heavens and the earth, the seas, and the fountains of waters; to believe in his Son, Jesus Christ, repenting of their sins, to be baptized for the remission of the same; and then we have promised them the Holy Ghost. In doing this the Lord has stood by us, sustaining those principles that we have advanced; and when we have ministered unto men the ordinances of the gospel; they have received for themselves the witness of the Spirit, even the Holy Ghost, making known to them for a surety that the principles that they had received were from God. (John Taylor, *The Gospel Kingdom: Selections from the Writings and Discourses of John Taylor*, ed. G. Homer Durham [1943], 223)

Prophets Have Admonished Us to Proclaim the Gospel

Missionary work is a work of love and trust, and it has to be done on that basis.

Be a part of this great process which constantly adds to the vitality of the Church. Every time a new member comes into the Church, something happens. There is an infusion of strength and faith and testimony that is wonderful. Think of what this Church would be without the missionary program.

Think of it! I think this is the greatest age in the history of the world. I think this is the greatest time in the history of the Church. I believe that. I think there will be greater times in the future. We are growing ever and ever stronger. . . .

What a responsibility we have. The whole fate of the world depends on us, according to the revelations of the Almighty. We cannot waste time. We cannot be unrighteous in our living. We cannot let our thoughts dwell on immoral things. We have to be the very best that we can be, you and I, because the very relationship of God our Eternal Father to His children on the earth depends on their accepting what we have come to teach according to His magnificent word. (Gordon B. Hinckley, *Teachings of Gordon B. Hinckley* [1997], 374–75)

Prophets Have Admonished Us to Proclaim the Gospel

There can be no greater or more important calling for men than that in which the Elders of the Church of Jesus Christ of Latterday Saints are engaged, when in the discharge of their duties as missionaries to the world. They stand as teachers, counselors and leaders to the people. They are commissioned with the word of life, and "the power of God unto salvation," to minister unto this proud, conceited, selfrighteous, but benighted and degenerate world. (Joseph F. Smith, "The Sacredness of Our Calling," *Millennial Star*, June 28, 1875, 408)

President Heber J. Grant taught us: "The missionary work of the Latterday Saints is the greatest of all the great works in all the world" (in Conference Report, Oct. 1921, 5).

Our Great Responsibility Is to Preach the Gospel

The Lord has defined certain great responsibilities for His Church. He said as one of the signs of His coming that the gospel of the kingdom was to be preached unto all the world for a witness unto all nations, and then should the end come, or the destruction of the wicked (see Matthew 24:14). That witness, we have understood, was to be a witness of the mission of the Messiah. It was to be a witness of the divinity of His mission. It was to be a witness that the gospel of Jesus Christ had been restored in all its fulness in this, the dispensation of the fulness of times. (Harold B. Lee, *The Teachings of Harold B. Lee*, ed. Clyde J. Williams [1996], 595)

Prophets Have Admonished Us to Proclaim the Gospel

Our missionaries are going forth to different nations, and in Germany, Palestine, New Holland, Australia, the East Indies, and other places, the Standard of Truth has been erected; no unhallowed hand can stop the work from progressing; persecutions may rage, mobs may combine, armies may assemble, calumny may defame, but the truth of God will go forth boldly, nobly, and independent, till it has penetrated every continent, visited every clime, swept every country, and sounded in every ear, till the purposes of God shall be accomplished, and the Great Jehovah shall say the work is done. (Joseph Smith, in *History of the Church*, 4:540)

The Joy of Proclaiming the Gospel

I know that which the Lord hath commanded me, and I glory in it. I do not glory of myself, but I glory in that which the Lord hath commanded me; yea, and this is my glory, that perhaps I may be an instrument in the hands of God to bring some soul to repentance; and this is my joy.

And behold, when I see many of my brethren truly penitent, and coming to the Lord their God, then is my soul filled with joy. (Alma 29:9–10)

And now, behold, I say unto you, that the thing which will be of the most worth unto you will be to declare repentance unto this people, that you may bring souls unto me, that you may rest with them in the kingdom of my Father. Amen. (D&C 15:6)

The Worth of Souls Is Great

Remember the worth of souls is great in the sight of God;

For, behold, the Lord your Redeemer suffered death in the flesh; wherefore he suffered the pain of all men, that all men might repent and come unto him.

And he hath risen again from the dead, that he might bring all men unto him, on conditions of repentance.

And how great is his joy in the soul that repenteth!

Wherefore, you are called to cry repentance unto this people.

And if it so be that you should labor all your days in crying repentance unto this people, and bring, save it be one soul unto me, how great shall be your joy with him in the kingdom of my Father!

And now, if your joy will be great with one soul that you have brought unto me into the kingdom of my Father, how great will be your joy if you should bring many souls unto me! (D&C 18:10–16)

Missionary Work Brings Salvation to Our Souls

"For behold the field is white already to harvest; and lo, he that thrusteth in his sickle with his might, the same layeth up in store that he perisheth not, but bringeth salvation to his soul" (D&C 4:4). In other words, no man ever puts out his hand to help another without gaining for himself the right to a merited salvation because of his willingness to help others. Now, keep in mind that all of us are our Father's children, whether presently members of the Church or not. It is these others of our Father's children about whom we must be much concerned. They are just as dear to Him as those who are presently members of the Church. If any one of us sets himself to the task of bringing others into the fold, the Lord says he brings salvation to his own soul. (Harold B. Lee, *The Teachings of Harold B. Lee*, ed. Clyde J. Williams [1996], 594)

Prophets Have Encouraged Us to Prepare Well

First, *prepare with purpose*. Remember the qualifying statement of the Master: "Behold, the Lord requireth the heart and a willing mind." . . . No other labor requires longer hours or greater devotion or such sacrifice and fervent prayer.

Second, *teach with testimony*. Peter and John, those converted fishermen who became Apostles, were warned not to preach Jesus Christ and Him crucified. Their answer was firm: "Whether it be right in the sight of God to hearken unto you more than unto God, judge ye. For we cannot but speak the things which we have seen and heard."

Third, *labor with love*. There is no substitute for love. . . . "And faith, hope, charity and love, with an eye single to the glory of God, qualify him for the work." . . . When our lives comply with God's standard and we labor with love to bring souls unto Him, those within our sphere of influence will never speak the lament, "The harvest is past, the summer is ended, and we are not saved." (Thomas S. Monson, "President Monson: Missionary Work," lds.org)

Your Missionary Commission

I am called of God. My authority is above that of the kings of the earth. By revelation I have been selected as a personal representative of the Lord Jesus Christ. He is my Master and He has chosen me to represent Him. To stand in His place, to say and do what He himself would say and do if He personally were ministering to the very people to whom He has sent me. My voice is His voice, and my acts are His acts; my words are His words and my doctrine is His doctrine. My commission is to do what He wants done. To say what He wants said. To be a living modern witness in word and deed of the divinity of His great and marvelous latter-day work. (Bruce R. McConkie, "How Great Is My Calling," address delivered while serving as president of the Australian Mission, 1961–64)

The Greatest Work in All the World

There are at least twenty-seven sections of the Doctrine and Covenants that refer to missionary work. The first great responsibility placed upon this Church in our day was to carry this message to the world. It is still a major responsibility. It is going on here on earth and it is going on in greater volume on the other side, and whether you do it here or over there doesn't make very much difference, just so long as you are missionaries. If you are laboring as you should, if you love this work, you will be engaged in helping to save the souls of the children of man throughout eternity until they have all heard it. And so it is the greatest work in all the world. There isn't anything like it in magnitude, in importance, in size, in promise. (Ezra Taft Benson, *The Teachings of Ezra Taft Benson* [1988], 186)

Desire to Serve the Lord

Actually, everything depends—initially and finally—on our desires. These shape our thought patterns. Our desires thus precede our deeds and lie at the very cores of our souls, tilting us toward or away from God (see D&C 4:3). God can "educate our desires." Others seek to manipulate our desires. But it is we who form the desires, the "thoughts and intents of [our] hearts" (Mosiah 5:13).

The end rule is "according to [our] desires . . . shall it be done unto [us]" (D&C 11:17), "for I, the Lord, will judge all men according to their works, according to the desire of their hearts" (D&C 137:9; see also Alma 41:5; D&C 6:20, 27). A person's individual will thus remains uniquely his. God will not override it or overwhelm it. Hence we'd better want the consequences of what we want! . . .

But we must desire and provide it. (Neal A. Maxwell, *If Thou Endure It Well* [1996], 51)

The Missionary Spirit

I have waded swamps and swum rivers, and have asked my bread from door to door; and have devoted nearly fifty years to this work. And why? Was there gold enough in California to have hired me to do it? No, verily; and what I have done and what my brethren have done, we have done because we were commanded of God. And this is the position we occupy today. We have preached and labored at home and abroad, and we intend to continue our labors, by the help of God, as long as we can have liberty to do it, and until the Gentiles prove themselves unworthy of eternal life, and until the judgments of God overtake the world, which are at the door. (Wilford Woodruff, in *Journal of Discourses*, 23:130)

Heavenly Father Answers Our Prayers

A missionary learns that God, our Heavenly Father, can and does answer prayers. He learns to recognize the promptings of the Holy Spirit and to be directed by that Spirit. He prays for his own welfare—to be humble and susceptible to the influence of the Holy Ghost—as well as for the people with whom he is laboring. Through these experiences of prayer and service, he learns to love the Lord with all his heart and to more fully love his fellowmen. (Ezra Taft Benson, *The Teachings of Ezra Taft Benson* [1988], 182)

The Power of Prayer

Behold, verily, verily, I say unto you, ye must watch and pray always lest ye enter into temptation; for Satan desireth to have you, that he may sift you as wheat. (3 Nephi 18:18)

Nevertheless the children of God were commanded that they should gather themselves together oft, and join in fasting and mighty prayer in behalf of the welfare of the souls of those who knew not God. (Alma 6:6)

But this is not all; they had given themselves to much prayer, and fasting; therefore they had the spirit of prophecy, and the spirit of revelation, and when they taught, they taught with power and authority of God. (Alma 17:3)

And the Spirit shall be given unto you by the prayer of faith; and if ye receive not the Spirit ye shall not teach. (D&C 42:14)

Born of the Word of God

Men must first be born of the word of God, which lives and abides for ever. As the Apostle Peter says, "being born again, not of corruptible seed, but of incorruptible, by the word of God, which liveth and abideth forever." The Apostle James says, "Of his own will begat He us with the word of truth." And again we read, "Faith cometh by hearing the word of God." God's way is this: "He calls men who are fitted for His work, and inspires them, and endows them with authority to represent Him, and sends them forth to preach the word of God. . . . The word spoken by the gift and power of God carries conviction to the heart, and they at once begin to recognize the authority of Him who imparts the words of life to them. They are born of the word and are able to see and understand to a certain degree, their faith and their ideas having been quickened by the power of God. (Charles W. Penrose, in *Journal of Discourses*, 23:350)

The Lord Will Help You

Your greatest help will come from the Lord Himself as you supplicate and plead with Him in humble prayer. As you are driven to your knees again and again, asking Him for divine help in your mission, you will feel the Spirit, you will get your answer from above, your mission will prosper spiritually because of your dependence and your reliance on Him.

The modern-day challenging and testifying missionary prays every morning to "lead me this day to a family that I can fulfil my purpose." (Ezra Taft Benson, *The Teachings of Ezra Taft Benson* [1988], 199–200)

Christ Is the Good Shepherd

Christ is the Shepherd (Genesis 49:24; Psalms. 23; 1 Peter 2:25; Mormon 5:17), the Chief Shepherd

(1 Peter 5:4), the Great Shepherd (Hebrews 13:20), the True Shepherd (Helaman 15:13), the Shepherd of Israel (Psalms 80:1), the Good Shepherd. (D&C 50:44; John 10:7–18; Alma 5:38–60; Helaman 7:18) His saints are the sheep; his sheepfold is the Church of Jesus Christ; and the day will come when there will be "one God and one Shepherd over all the earth" (1 Nephi 13:41), "and he shall feed his sheep, and in him they shall find pasture." (1 Nephi 22:25) . . .

The parable of the lost sheep (Matthew 18:12–13; Luke 15:3–7) and the commands: "Feed my lambs. . . . Feed my sheep" (John 21:15–17) exemplify the standing orders he has given his other shepherds. (Bruce R. McConkie, *Mormon Doctrine*, 2nd ed. [1966], 328)

Trust in the Lord

Trust in the Lord with all thine heart; and lean not unto thine own understanding. In all thy ways acknowledge him, and he shall direct thy paths. (Proverbs 3:5–6)

Yea, I know that I am nothing; as to my strength I am weak; therefore I will not boast of myself, but I will boast of my God, for in his strength I can do all things; yea, behold, many mighty miracles we have wrought in this land, for which we will praise his name forever. (Alma 26:12)

And now, O my son Helaman, behold, thou art in thy youth, and therefore, I beseech of thee that thou wilt hear my words and learn of me; for I do know that whosoever shall put their trust in God shall be supported in their trials, and their troubles, and their afflictions, and shall be lifted up at the last day. (Alma 36:3)

The Prophets Admonish Us to Trust in the Lord

We must be a tried people. We must walk by faith, putting our trust in the Lord and not, at present, by sight. In this way the leaders of the people of God, as well as the people themselves, have their faith tested. (George Q. Cannon, *Gospel Truth: Discourses and Writings of President George Q. Cannon*, ed. Jerreld L. Newquist [1957], 300)

Accept responsibility in the Church, and trust in the Lord to make you equal to any call you may receive. Your example will set a pattern for your children. Reach out in love to those in distress and need. (Gordon B. Hinckley, *Teachings of Gordon B. Hinckley* [1997], 391)

The Lord Is the Only Way—Come Follow Him

The Master could be found mingling with the poor, the downtrodden, the oppressed, and the afflicted. He brought hope to the hopeless, strength to the weak, and freedom to the captive. He taught of the better life to come—even eternal life. This knowledge ever directs those who receive the divine injunction, "Follow thou me." It guided Peter. It motivated Paul. It can determine our personal destiny. Can we make the decision to follow in righteousness and truth the Redeemer of the world? With His help, a rebellious boy can become an obedient man, a wayward girl can cast aside the old self and begin anew. Indeed, the gospel of Jesus Christ can change men's lives. (Thomas S. Monson, in *Conference Classics*, 3 vols. [1981–84], 2:67)

Center Our Lives on Christ

If our lives are centered in Christ, nothing can go permanently wrong. I am aware that life presents many challenges, but with the help of the Lord, we need not fear. If our lives and our faith are centered on Jesus Christ and his restored gospel, nothing can ever go permanently wrong. On the other hand, if our lives are not centered on the Savior and his teachings, no other success can ever be permanently right. (Howard W. Hunter, *The Teachings of Howard W. Hunter*, ed. by Clyde J. Williams [1997], 40; italics added)

Worship the Lord in All That You Do

The prayer (the Lord's Prayer) closes with these beautiful words of adoration and praise, "For thine is the kingdom, the power and the glory forever." Let us look upon this prayer as teaching us true worship. We come together to worship the Lord both in prayer, in preaching, in praising the Lord, and in singing inspired hymns. We do adore Him who is our Creator and our Father. We know He is all-good, all-wise and all-powerful, and worthy of all praise, and we rejoice in the promise given us that He will hear and answer our prayers. (Anthon H. Lund, in Conference Report, Oct. 1914, 13)

Feast upon the Word of God

We hope that you are studying the gospel regularly. Read from the scriptures, especially the Book of Mormon, each day as individuals and as families.

Study the word of the Lord, and your faith and testimony will increase. What could be a more profitable use of discretionary time than reading from the scriptural library, the literature that teaches us to know God and understand our relationship to him? . . .

Not in this dispensation, surely not in any dispensation, have the scriptures—the enduring, enlightening word of God—been so readily available and so helpfully structured for the use of every man, woman, and child who will search them. The written word of God is in the most readable and accessible form ever provided to lay members in the history of the world. Surely we will be held accountable if we do not read them. (Howard W. Hunter, *The Teachings of Howard W. Hunter*, ed. Clyde J. Williams [1997], 51)

The Word of God Will Tell Us All Things to Do

Angels speak by the power of the Holy Ghost; wherefore, they speak the words of Christ. Wherefore, I said unto you, feast upon the words of Christ; for behold, the words of Christ will tell you all things what ye should do. (2 Nephi 32:3)

Therefore, as we search the scriptures, our focus should be upon that which will tell us what we must do (to become as He is) and upon that which will stir us so to do. And the very word *search* means from the beginning to the latest unfolding of Holy Writ. (Neal A. Maxwell, *Even As I Am* [1982], 19)

Live with a Grateful Heart

That ye contend no more against the Holy Ghost, but that ye receive it, and take upon you the name of Christ; that ye humble yourselves even to the dust, and worship God, in whatsoever place ye may be in, in spirit and in truth; and that ye live in thanksgiving daily, for the many mercies and blessings which he doth bestow upon you. (Alma 34:38)

I say unto you, my brethren, that if you should render all the thanks and praise which your whole soul has power to possess, to that God who has created you, and has kept and preserved you, and has caused that ye should rejoice, and has granted that ye should live in peace one with another—

I say unto you that if ye should serve him who has created you from the beginning, and is preserving you from day to day, by lending you breath, that ye may live and move and do according to your own will, and even supporting you from one moment to another—I say, if ye should serve him with all your whole souls yet ye would be unprofitable servants. (Mosiah 2:20–21)

The Sin of Ingratitude

The Prophet Joseph is reported to have said at one time that one of the greatest sins for which the Latter-day Saints would be guilty would be the sin of ingratitude. . . . Sometimes I feel we need to devote more of our prayers to expressions of gratitude and thanksgiving for blessings already received. (Ezra Taft Benson, *The Teachings of Ezra Taft Benson* [1988], 363)

I do not know of any, excepting the unpardonable sin, that is greater than the sin of ingratitude. (Brigham Young, *Discourses of Brigham Young*, sel. John A. Widtsoe [1954], 228)

Expressing Gratitude

Our society is afflicted by a spirit of thoughtless arrogance unbecoming those who have been so magnificently blessed. How grateful we should be for the bounties we enjoy. Absence of gratitude is the mark of the narrow, uneducated mind. It bespeaks a lack of knowledge and the ignorance of self-sufficiency. It expresses itself in ugly egotism and frequently in wanton mischief. . . .

Where there is appreciation, there is courtesy, there is concern for the rights and property of others. Without appreciation, there is arrogance and evil. (Gordon B. Hinckley, *Teachings of Gordon B. Hinckley* [1997], 247)

Gratitude Sees the Good

The grateful man sees so much in the world to be thankful for, and with him the good outweighs the evil. Love overpowers jealousy, and light drives darkness out of his life. Pride destroys our gratitude and sets up selfishness in its place. How much happier we are in the presence of a grateful and loving soul, and how careful we should be to cultivate, through the medium of a prayerful life, a thankful attitude toward God and man! (Joseph F. Smith, *Gospel Doctrine: Selections from the Sermons and Writings of Joseph F. Smith*, comp. John A. Widtsoe [1919], 263)

Understanding and Appreciating the Infinite Atonement

No member of this Church must ever forget the terrible price paid by our Redeemer who gave his life that all men might live—the agony of Gethsemane, the bitter mockery of his trial, the vicious crown of thorns tearing at his flesh, the blood cry of the mob before Pilate, the lonely burden of his heavy walk along the way to Calvary, the terrifying pain as great nails pierced his hands and feet, the fevered torture of his body as he hung that tragic day, the Son of God crying out, "Father, forgive them; for they know not what they do." (Luke 23:34) . . .

We cannot forget that. We must never forget it, for here our Savior, our Redeemer, the Son of God, gave himself a vicarious sacrifice for each of us. . . .

Everything depended on Him—His atoning sacrifice. . . . He faced it. . . . It is beyond our comprehension, I believe. Nevertheless, we glimpse it in small part and must learn to appreciate it more and more and more. (Gordon B. Hinckley, *Teachings of Gordon B. Hinckley* [1997], 26–27, 30)

The Atonement Succors Us

And he cometh into the world that he may save all men if they will hearken unto his voice; for behold, he suffereth the pains of all men, yea, the pains of every living creature, both men, women, and children, who belong to the family of Adam.

And he suffereth this that the resurrection might pass upon all men, that all might stand before him at the great and judgment day. (2 Nephi 9:21–22)

And he shall go forth, suffering pains and afflictions and temptations of every kind; and this that the word might be fulfilled which saith he will take upon him the pains and the sicknesses of his people.

And he will take upon him death, that he may loose the bands of death which bind his people; and he will take upon him their infirmities, that his bowels may be filled with mercy, according to the flesh, that he may know according to the flesh how to succor his people according to their infirmities. (Alma 7:11–12)

How Does the Atonement Relate to Missionary Work?

Any time we experience the blessings of the Atonement in our lives, we cannot help but have a concern for the welfare of our brethren.

Examples abound in the Book of Mormon that illustrate this principle. When Lehi partook of the fruit of the tree, symbolic of partaking of the Atonement, he said, "I began to be desirous that my family should partake" (1 Nephi 8:12). When Enos experienced his conversion and received a forgiveness of his sins, because of his faith in Jesus Christ he said, "I began to feel a desire for the welfare of my brethren, the Nephites" (Enos 1:9). Then he prayed for the Lamanites, the implacable enemies to the Nephites. Then there is the example of the four sons of Mosiah—Ammon, Aaron, Omner, and Himni—who received a forgiveness of sins through the Atonement and then labored for years among the Lamanites to bring them to Christ. The record states that they could not bear the thought that any soul should perish (see Mosiah 28:3). (Howard W. Hunter, *The Teachings of Howard W. Hunter*, ed. Clyde J. Williams [1997], 248–49)

Offer All as a Sacrifice and Please Heavenly Father

Let us here observe, that a religion that does not require the sacrifice of all things never has power sufficient to produce the faith necessary unto life and salvation; for, from the first existence of man, the faith necessary unto the enjoyment of life and salvation never could be obtained without the sacrifice of all earthly things. It was through this sacrifice, and this only, that God has ordained that men should enjoy eternal life; and it is through the medium of the sacrifice of all earthly things that men do actually know that they are doing the things that are well pleasing in the sight of God. (Joseph Smith, *Lectures on Faith* [1985], 6:7)

Blessings to the Lord's Covenant People

Now if we keep the laws and covenants of baptism, and honor the priesthood and its covenants, we are then permitted to enter into the temple of the Lord and there again make covenants with him, which covenants if kept will qualify us for the fullness of joy in our Father's kingdom; and to become endowed with powers, rights, blessings, and promises of blessings that may embellish our lives and bless us eternally and bring us joy that is beyond our power to comprehend. . . .

We are indeed a covenant-making people. I hope and pray that we are also a covenant-keeping people. Unspeakable joy, indescribable blessings and associations with those that we love await all who receive the covenants of God and who endure to the end, faithful and true.For—

Eye hath not seen, nor ear heard, neither have entered into the heart of man, the things which God hath prepared for them that love him. (1 Corinthians 2:9) (Elray L. Christiansen, in Conference Report, Apr. 1955, 30)

Increase in Your Faith

Nevertheless they did fast and pray oft, and did wax stronger and stronger in their humility, and firmer and firmer in the faith of Christ, unto the filling their souls with joy and consolation, yea, even to the purifying and the sanctification of their hearts, which sanctification cometh because of their yielding their hearts unto God. (Helaman 3:35)

So then faith cometh by hearing, and hearing by the word of God. (Romans 10:17)

If there is any one thing you and I need in this world it is faith, that dynamic, powerful, marvelous element by which, as Paul declared, the very worlds were framed (Hebrews 11:3). . . . Faith—the kind of faith that moves one to get on his knees and plead with the Lord and then get on his feet and go to work—is an asset beyond compare, even in the acquisition of secular knowledge. (Gordon B. Hinckley, *Teachings of Gordon B. Hinckley* [1997], 186)

Faith Is the Power to Do All Things

Now let me describe to you what faith in Jesus Christ means. Faith in Him is more than mere acknowledgment that He lives. It is more than professing belief. Faith in Jesus Christ consists of complete reliance on Him. As God, He has infinite power, intelligence, and love. There is no human problem beyond His capacity to solve. Because He descended below all things, He knows how to help us rise above our daily difficulties. (Ezra Taft Benson, *The Teachings of Ezra Taft Benson* [1988], 66)

Behold, it was the faith of Ammon and his brethren which wrought so great a miracle among the Lamanites.

Yea, and even all they who wrought miracles wrought them by faith, even those who were before Christ and also those who were after.

And it was by faith that the three disciples obtained a promise that they should not taste of death; and they obtained not the promise until after their faith.

And neither at any time hath any wrought miracles until after their faith; wherefore they first believed in the Son of God. (Ether 12:15–18)

Live with Hope

Wherefore, whoso believeth in God might with surety hope for a better world, yea, even a place at the right hand of God, which hope cometh of faith, maketh an anchor to the souls of men, which would make them sure and steadfast, always abounding in good works, being led to glorify God. (Ether 12:4)

Wherefore, ye must press forward with a steadfastness in Christ, having a perfect brightness of hope, and a love of God and of all men. Wherefore, if ye shall press forward, feasting upon the word of Christ, and endure to the end, behold, thus saith the Father: Ye shall have eternal life. (2 Nephi 31:20)

> And what is it that ye shall hope for? Behold I say unto you that ye shall have hope through the atonement of Christ and the power of his resurrection, to be raised unto life eternal, and this because of your faith in him according to the promise. (Moroni 7:41)

Empowering Nature of Hope

> Hope has a greater circumference than faith. If faith increases, the perimeter of hope stretches correspondingly. (Neal A. Maxwell, "Brightness of Hope," *Ensign*, Oct. 1994)

Real hope, said Paul, is a hope for things that are not seen that are true (see Romans 8:24). Paul accurately linked hopelessness and godlessness as he wrote of those "having no hope, and without God in the world" (Ephesians 2:12). Christ-centered hope, however, is a very specific and particularized hope. It is focused on the great realities of the resurrection, eternal life, a better world, and Christ's triumphant second coming "things as they really will be." (Jacob 4:13; italics added) (Neal A. Maxwell, *Notwithstanding My Weakness* [1981], 40–41)

Charity Never Faileth

If a man be meek and lowly in heart, and confesses by the power of the Holy Ghost that Jesus is the Christ, he must needs have charity; for if he have not charity he is nothing; wherefore he must needs have charity.

And charity suffereth long, and is kind, and envieth not, and is not puffed up, seeketh not her own, is not easily provoked, thinketh no evil, and rejoiceth not in iniquity but rejoiceth in the truth, beareth all things, believeth all things, hopeth all things, endureth all things.

Wherefore, my beloved brethren, if ye have not charity, ye are nothing, for charity never faileth. Wherefore, cleave unto charity, which is the greatest of all, for all things must fail. (Moroni 7:44–46)

Charity—The Crowning Virtue

And now I know that this love which thou hast had for the children of men is charity; wherefore, except men shall have charity they cannot inherit that place which thou hast prepared in the mansions of thy Father. (Ether 12:34)

The final and crowning virtue of the divine character is *charity*, or the pure love of Christ (see Moroni 7:47). If we would truly seek to be more like our Savior and Master, then learning to love as He loves should be our highest goal. Mormon called charity "the greatest of all." (Moroni 7:46) (Ezra Taft Benson, "Godly Characteristics of the Master," *Ensign*, Nov. 1986, 45)

Seek to Possess Charity

> But charity is the pure love of Christ, and it endureth forever; and whoso is found possessed of it at the last day, it shall be well with him. Wherefore, my beloved brethren, pray unto the Father with all the energy of heart, that ye may be filled with this love, which he hath bestowed upon all who are true followers of his Son, Jesus Christ; that ye may become the sons of God; that when he shall appear we shall be like him, for we shall see him as he is; that we may have this hope; that we may be purified even as he is pure. Amen. (Moroni 7:47–48)

Love is one of the chief characteristics of Deity, and ought to be manifested by those who aspire to be the sons of God. A man filled with the love of God, is not content with blessing his family alone, but ranges through the whole world, anxious to bless the whole human race. (Joseph Smith, in *History of the Church*, 4:227)

The Greatest Missionary Tool

As missionaries, you must learn to love the scriptures. Your purpose for being in the mission field is to save souls, to baptize converts, to bring converted families into the Lord's Church. I ask you to give particular attention to scriptures which explain your holy calling, such as Doctrine and Covenants sections 4, 11, 15, 16, and 18, and the Book of Mormon. . . .

The Book of Mormon is for both member and nonmember. Combined with the Spirit of the Lord, the Book of Mormon is the greatest single tool which God has given us to convert the world. If we are to have the harvest of souls, we must use the instrument which God has designed for that task—the Book of Mormon. (Ezra Taft Benson, *The Teachings of Ezra Taft Benson* [1988], 204–5)

Strengthening Your Converts

There is a difference between a convert who is built on the rock of Christ through the Book of Mormon and stays hold of the iron rod, and one who is not. I promise you that you will have more and better converts in every mission of the Church if you will teach and inspire missionaries to effectively use the Book of Mormon as the great converter. (Ezra Taft Benson, *The Teachings of Ezra Taft Benson* [1988], 203–4)

Love the Book of Mormon

We need missionaries to match our message. We need missionaries who really know and love the Book of Mormon, who have a burning testimony of its divinity, and who by the Spirit can challenge their investigators to read and ponder its pages, knowing with complete assurance that the Lord will manifest the truth of the Book of Mormon to them by the power of the Holy Ghost. . . .

A missionary who is inspired by the Spirit of the Lord must be led by that Spirit to choose the proper approach to be effective. We must not forget that the Lord Himself provided the Book of Mormon as His chief witness. The Book of Mormon is still our most powerful missionary tool. Let us use it. (Ezra Taft Benson, *The Teachings of Ezra Taft Benson* [1988], 204)

What Greater Calling

What greater calling can any man have on the face of the earth than to hold in his hands power and authority to go forth and administer in the ordinances of salvation? Do we prize these things in their fullness? I do not think we do. Nevertheless, so far we have been enabled to maintain our position, and to go forth and fulfil our missions as far as we have had time and opportunity. Certainly there has been nothing in this work that I have had greater consolation in than in preaching the Gospel to my fellow men and in administering unto them the ordinances of the house of God, both for the living and the dead. (Wilford Woodruff, *Millennial Star*, May 14, 1896, 58:307)

Preach Faith unto Repentance

And thus he shall bring salvation to all those who shall believe on his name; this being the intent of this last sacrifice, to bring about the bowels of mercy, which overpowereth justice, and bringeth about means unto men that they may have faith unto repentance.

And thus mercy can satisfy the demands of justice, and encircles them in the arms of safety, while he that exercises no faith unto repentance is exposed to the whole law of the demands of justice; therefore only unto him that has faith unto repentance is brought about the great and eternal plan of redemption.

Therefore may God grant unto you, my brethren, that ye may begin to exercise your faith unto repentance, that ye begin to call upon his holy name, that he would have mercy upon you. (Alma 34:15–17)

Preach the Gospel

Some may wonder why General Authorities speak of the same things from conference to conference. As I study the utterances of the prophets through the centuries, their pattern is very clear. We seek, in the words of Alma, to teach people an everlasting hatred against sin and iniquity. We preach "repentance, and faith on the Lord Jesus Christ." (Alma 37:32, 33) We praise humility. We seek to teach people "to withstand every temptation of the devil, with their faith on the Lord Jesus Christ." (Alma 37:33) We teach our people "to never be weary of good works." (Alma 37:34) (Spencer W. Kimball, "The Stone Cut without Hands," *Ensign*, May 1976, 4)

Repent or We Must Suffer for Our Sins

Therefore I command you to repent—repent, lest I smite you by the rod of my mouth, and by my wrath, and by my anger, and your sufferings be sore—how sore you know not, how exquisite you know not, yea, how hard to bear you know not.

For behold, I, God, have suffered these things for all, that they might not suffer if they would repent;

But if they would not repent they must suffer even as I;

Which suffering caused myself, even God, the greatest of all, to tremble because of pain, and to bleed at every pore, and to suffer both body and spirit—and would that I might not drink the bitter cup, and shrink—

Nevertheless, glory be to the Father, and I partook and finished my preparations unto the children of men. (D&C 19:15–19)

Repentance Is the Only Way to Christ

In order for good to blossom it must be cultivated and exercised by constant practice, and to be truly righteous there is required a daily pruning of the evil growth of our characters by a daily repentance from sin. (Harold B. Lee, *The Teachings of Harold B. Lee*, ed. Clyde J. Williams [1996], 113)

Repentance is one of the first principles of the gospel. Forgiveness is a mark of divinity. There is hope for you. Your lives are ahead, and they can be filled with happiness, even though the past may have been marred by sin. This is a work of saving and assisting people with their problems. This is the purpose of the gospel. (Gordon B. Hinckley, *Teachings of Gordon B. Hinckley* [1997], 548)

Baptism Is Accepting Christ—The Lord Wants Baptisms

And whoso believeth in me, and is baptized, the same shall be saved; and they are they who shall inherit the kingdom of God.

And whoso believeth not in me, and is not baptized, shall be damned. (3 Nephi 11:33–34)

And again I say unto you, ye must repent, and become as a little child, and be baptized in my name, or ye can in nowise receive these things.

And again I say unto you, ye must repent, and be baptized in my name, and become as a little child, or ye can in nowise inherit the kingdom of God. (3 Nephi 11:37–38)

Verily I say unto you, that whoso repenteth of his sins through your words, and desireth to be baptized in my name, on this wise shall ye baptize them—Behold, ye shall go down and stand in the water, and in my name shall ye baptize them. (3 Nephi 11:23)

Four Things to Emphasize as a Missionary

I testify to you of the truthfulness of these four great points of emphasis on missionary work. First, the sacredness of saving souls and the importance of greatly increasing the number of convert baptisms. Second, the necessity of increasing our own personal faith in order that convert baptisms will increase in a significant and dramatic way. Third, the importance of missionaries prayerfully and with the Spirit setting personal convert baptismal goals. Fourth, the urgency of being actively and productively engaged in member-missionary work in order that the Lord's harvest may be accomplished. (Ezra Taft Benson, *The Teachings of Ezra Taft Benson* [1988], 186)

Saving Souls Is the Greatest Work

Missionaries are engaged in the greatest work in all the world—saving the souls of our Father in Heaven's children. They have been called by inspiration and revelation at this time for a sacred and holy purpose. They are serving exactly where the Lord wants them, for them they are in the best mission of the Church, they cannot fail in this work, they have been called to succeed, and succeed they will. (Ezra Taft Benson, *The Teachings of Ezra Taft Benson* [1988], 189–90)

Missionaries Are on the Lord's Errand

Let me give you a scripture that indicates just how close the Lord wants to be to us in our work. In section 64, verse 29, the Lord says this: "Wherefore, as ye are agents, ye are on the Lord's errand; and whatever ye do according to the will of the Lord is the Lord's business." Every one of you has been made an agent of the Lord by the laying on of hands. You have been given a commission. Because of that commission, each one of you is on an errand. You are on the Lord's errand. Whatever you do according to the will of the Lord, it is His business. He wants you to make it His business. He is going to stay by you. He is going to help you. He is going to direct you. (Harold B. Lee, *The Teachings of Harold B. Lee*, ed. Clyde J. Williams [1996], 596)

Follow the Son of God

Let us follow the Son of God in all ways and in all walks of life. Let us make him our exemplar and our guide. We should at every opportunity ask ourselves, "What would Jesus do?" and then be more courageous to act upon the answer. We must follow Christ, in the best sense of that word. We must be about his work as he was about his Father's. We should try to be like him, even as the Primary children sing, "Try, try, try" (*Children's Songbook*, p. 55). To the extent that our mortal powers permit, we should make every effort to become like Christ—the one perfect and sinless example this world has ever seen. (Howard W. Hunter, *The Teachings of Howard W. Hunter*, ed. Clyde J. Williams [1997], 43)

The Blessings of the Holy Ghost

Regarding the Holy Ghost, the prophet Wilford Woodruff said, "You may have the administration of angels; you may see many miracles; you may see many wonders in the earth; but I claim that the gift of the Holy Ghost is the greatest gift that can be bestowed upon man" (*Deseret Weekly*, Apr. 6, 1889, 451).

The prophet Brigham Young likewise emphasized the blessing of the companionship of the Holy Ghost when he said, "If the Latter-day Saints will walk up to their privileges and exercise faith in the name of Jesus Christ and live in the enjoyment of the fullness of the Holy Ghost constantly day by day, there is nothing on the face of the earth that they could ask for, that would not be given to them. The Lord is waiting to be very gracious unto this people, and to pour out upon them riches, honor, glory, and power, even that they may possess all things according to the promises He has made through His apostles and prophets." (in *Journal of Discourses*, 11:114)

Prepare to Have the Companionship of the Holy Ghost

The Prophet Joseph Smith appeared to Brigham Young and said: "Tell the people to be humble and faithful, and be sure to keep the spirit of the Lord and it will lead them right. Be careful and not turn away the still small voice; it will teach you what to do and where to go; it will yield the fruits of the kingdom. Tell the brethren to keep their hearts open to conviction, so that when the Holy Ghost comes to them, their hearts will be ready to receive it." (*Manuscript History of Brigham Young: 1846–1847*, ed. Elden J. Watson [1971], 529)

[Lehi] spake by the power of the Holy Ghost, which power he received by faith on the Son of God. (1 Nephi 10:17)

They are only to be seen and understood by the power of the Holy Spirit, which God bestows on those who love him, and purify themselves before him. (D&C 76:116)

Always remember him and keep his commandments which he has given them; that they may always have his Spirit to be with them. (D&C 20:77)

The Power of the Holy Ghost

Only those who conform to the first ordinances of the gospel are connected officially with the powers of the Holy Ghost in such a way as to secure added help. A distinct and real power comes to the individual who receives the Holy Ghost. It is as if he had been given a key to a vast and wonderful building which he may enter at his pleasure. However, if the key be unused, the gift is of no value. Man must seek help from the Holy Ghost, if the gift shall be real. The gift of the Holy Ghost also represents a general law, for it is evident that all who have faith made active by repentance, and show obedience to law, will be in such harmony with intelligent forces as to receive much light from them if desired or needed. (John A. Widtsoe, *A Rational Theology* [1915], 96–97)

The Holy Ghost as a Constant Companion

"If you want to obtain and keep the guidance of the Spirit, you can do so by following this simple four-point program.

One, *pray.* Pray diligently. Pray with each other. Pray in public in the proper places. . . . Learn to talk to the Lord; call upon his name in great faith and confidence.

Second, *study* and learn the gospel.

Third, *live righteously*; repent of your sins by confessing them and forsaking them. Then conform to the teachings of the gospel.

Fourth, *give service* in the Church.

If you will do these things, you will get the guidance of the Holy Spirit and you will go through this world successfully, regardless of what the people of the world say or do." (Marion G. Romney, "Guidance of the Holy Spirit," *Ensign*, Jan. 1980, 5; italics added)

Preparing to Teach by the Holy Spirit

Now these sons of Mosiah were with Alma at the time the angel first appeared unto him; therefore Alma did rejoice exceedingly to see his brethren; and what added more to his joy, they were still his brethren in the Lord; yea, and they had waxed strong in the knowledge of the truth; for they were men of a sound understanding and they had searched the scriptures diligently, that they might know the word of God.

But this is not all; they had given themselves to much prayer, and fasting; therefore they had the spirit of prophecy, and the spirit of revelation, and when they taught, they taught with power and authority of God. (Alma 17:2–3)

Words to the Missionaries

I wish to say a few words to the missionaries—to those who are going abroad to preach the gospel of Christ. I want to give you a word of exhortation and counsel, brethren: that is, whenever you are in doubt about any duty or work which you have to perform, never proceed to do anything until you go and labour in prayer and get the Holy Spirit. Wherever the Spirit dictates you to go or to do, that will be right; and, by following its dictates, you will come out right. (Wilford Woodruff, in *Journal of Discourses*, 5:85)

Teaching with the Holy Spirit

And the Spirit shall be given unto you by the prayer of faith; and if ye receive not the Spirit ye shall not teach. (D&C 42:14)

Verily I say unto you, he that is ordained of me and sent forth to preach the word of truth by the Comforter, in the Spirit of truth, doth he preach it by the Spirit of truth or some other way?

And if it be by some other way it is not of God.

And again, he that receiveth the word of truth, doth he receive it by the Spirit of truth or some other way?

If it be some other way it is not of God.

Therefore, why is it that ye cannot understand and know, that he that receiveth the word by the Spirit of truth receiveth it as it is preached by the Spirit of truth?

Wherefore, he that preacheth and he that receiveth, understand one another, and both are edified and rejoice together. (D&C 50:17–22)

Conversion by the Power of the Holy Ghost

As missionaries, members are vital and necessary parts of the conversion process. Sometimes in our discussions of missionary work we state that a missionary "converts" so many persons. Actually, the missionary does not convert anyone: the Holy Ghost does the converting. The power of conversion is directly associated with the Holy Ghost, for no person can be truly converted and know that Jesus is the Christ save by the power of the Holy Ghost. (Spencer W. Kimball, *The Teachings of Spencer W. Kimball*, ed. Edward L. Kimball [1982], 570)

Missionaries—Do All You Can to Ensure That Converts Remain Faithful

You may recall that the sons of Mosiah were so effective in their teaching, with "the power of God working miracles in them," that "as many of the Lamanites as believed in their preaching, and were converted unto the Lord, never did fall away" (Alma 23:6). We trust that your efforts will be as fruitful. As you teach potential converts, make sure they have a sufficient foundation of faith, understanding, conviction, and commitment to keep themselves faithful when they become members of the Church. Please be certain there is coordination with the ward mission leader and stake missionaries so that new converts are warmly fellowshipped by ward or branch members. (Howard W. Hunter, *The Teachings of Howard W. Hunter*, ed. Clyde J. Williams [1997], 252)

Enduring to the End

Wherefore, if ye shall press forward, feasting upon the word of Christ, and endure to the end, behold, thus saith the Father: Ye shall have eternal life. (2 Nephi 31:20)

Often one hears trite, sometimes consciously apologetic references to "enduring to the end" as an addition to the first principles and ordinances of the gospel. Nevertheless, the doctrine of faithful endurance is infinitely serious, and it is here [2 Nephi 31:15–16] declared to be a basic principle of the gospel by the God and Father of us all. "Enduring to the end" is an integral element in the doctrine of Christ, and without it, it would have been better not to have known him. (Jeffrey R. Holland, *Christ and the New Covenant: The Messianic Message of the Book of Mormon* [1997], 54)

Enduring Well

Enduring affliction is certainly part of enduring to the end, but the word enduring also means to last, to continue, and to remain (see 2 Nephi 33:9). This emphasis on staying the course appears at so many points in the scriptures (for examples, see D&C 20:29; 2 Nephi 9:24). We could scarcely become "finished" or "completed" if we did not finish and complete all of life's assigned course! (Neal A. Maxwell, *Lord, Increase Our Faith* [1994], 45)

I know that each of us has much to do. Sometimes we feel overwhelmed by the tasks we face. But if we keep our priorities in order, we can accomplish all that we should. We can endure to the end regardless of temptations, problems, and challenges. Those who remain faithful will receive God's greatest blessing—eternal life—and the privilege of living with our Heavenly Father and his Beloved Son in the celestial kingdom. (Joseph B. Wirthlin, "The Straight and Narrow Way," *Ensign*, Nov. 1990, 64)

Adversity Is Part of Opposition in All Things

Our great purpose in life is to overcome adversity and worldly consideration as we strive for things of the Spirit. (Ezra Taft Benson, *The Teachings of Ezra Taft Benson* [1988], 449–50)

If as a people we will build and sustain one another, the Lord will bless us with the strength to weather every storm and continue to move forward through every adversity. (Gordon B. Hinckley, *Teachings of Gordon B. Hinckley* [1997], 7)

Many in today's generation have not fully known nor appreciated the refining blessings of adversity. Many have never been hungry because of want. Yet I am persuaded that there can be a necessary refining process in adversity that increases our understanding, enhances our sensitivity, makes us more Christlike. Lord Byron said, "Adversity is the first path to truth" (*Don Juan*, canto 12, stanza 50). The life of the Savior and the lives of His prophets clearly and simply teach how necessary adversity is to achieve a measure of greatness. (James E. Faust, "The Blessings of Adversity," *Liahona*, May 1998, 3)

Temptation and Choices

You constantly are faced with difficult choices. Your problems are not new, but they are intensified. You are subjected to temptations that are attractive and appealing. You represent the future of this Church, and the adversary of truth would like to injure you, would like to destroy your faith, would like to lead you down paths that are beguiling and interesting, but deadly. (Gordon B. Hinckley, *Teachings of Gordon B. Hinckley* [1997], 642–43)

To have strength to overcome temptation is Godlike. The strong, the virtuous and the true of every generation have lived pure, clean lives, not because their emotions were less impelling nor because their temptations were fewer but because their will to do was greater and their faith in divine guidance won them strength through prayer that proved their kinship with the great Exemplar who gave us the pattern for the perfect life. (Harold B. Lee, *Decisions for Successful Living* [1973], 43)

Missionaries Must Obey Mission Rules and Learn to Be Good Followers

We encourage you to obey the mission rules. Follow them specifically all the way through and you will be successful. You will learn that to be a leader you must first learn to be a good follower. You will never learn the principles of leadership until you learn how to follow them. You may feel that you know a lot more than your senior companion, but he is your senior companion and you should follow him in righteousness. This is one of the greatest lessons in life—to learn how to follow your district leader and zone leader and especially your mission president. (Howard W. Hunter, *The Teachings of Howard W. Hunter*, ed. Clyde J. Williams [1997], 252)

Lose Yourself in the Work

It is so important that you lose yourselves in this work, that you don't worry about "what is it going to do for me." You are not out in the world with self-improvement as the major objective, but you can't help getting a maximum amount of self-improvement if you lose yourself in the work of the Lord. I don't know of any better preparation for life than two years of devoted, unselfish, dedicated service as a missionary. (Ezra Taft Benson, *The Teachings of Ezra Taft Benson* [1988], 200–1)

Seek the Mind and Will of the Lord

I will take the liberty of saying that it is your privilege, brethren, to get the mind and will of the Lord in relation to your duties while abroad among the people; and it is also the privilege of the whole people who are called Israel to obtain the revelations of the Holy Spirit to guide them in every duty in life. Whatever position a man may stand in, it is his privilege, as a Saint of God, to enjoy this blessing; and a man who understands himself will not move without the operations of the Spirit to lead him. (Wilford Woodruff, in *Journal of Discourses*, 5:85)

The Atonement Enables Us to Avoid Temptation

A personal testimony of the Savior and his atonement can help us avoid temptation. Strive to build a personal testimony of Jesus Christ and the atonement. A study of the life of Christ and a testimony of his reality is something each of us should seek. As we come to understand his mission, and the atonement which he wrought, we will desire to live more like him. We especially encourage the young men and young women to come to know the reason for the atoning sacrifice of our Lord. When temptations come, as they surely will, an understanding of the Savior's agony in Gethsemane and his eventual death on the cross will be a reminder to you to avoid any activity that would cause the Savior more pain. Listen to his words, "For behold, I, God, have suffered these things for all, that they might not suffer if they would repent; But if they would not repent, they must suffer even as I" (D&C 19:16–17). (Howard W. Hunter, *The Teachings of Howard W. Hunter*, ed. Clyde J. Williams [1997], 31)

The Blessing and Accountability of Agency

Wherefore, the Lord God gave unto man that he should act for himself. Wherefore, man could not act for himself save it should be that he was enticed by the one or the other. (2 Nephi 2:16)

Wherefore, men are free according to the flesh; and all things are given them which are expedient unto man. And they are free to choose liberty and eternal life, through the great Mediator of all men, or to choose captivity and death, according to the captivity and power of the devil; for he seeketh that all men might be miserable like unto himself. (2 Nephi 2:27)

That every man may act in doctrine and principle pertaining to futurity, according to the moral agency which I have given unto him, that every man may be accountable for his own sins in the day of judgment. (D&C 101:78)

Agency Is Supreme

The volition of the creature is free; this is a law of their existence and the Lord cannot violate his own law; were he to do that, he would cease to be God. . . .

When the Lord made man, he made him an agent accountable to his God, with liberty to act and to do as he pleases to a certain extent in order to prove himself. (Brigham Young, *Discourses of Brigham Young*, sel. John A. Widtsoe [1954], 62)

There is the principle of God in every individual. It is designed that man should act as God, and not be constrained and controlled in everything, but have an independency, an agency and the power to spread abroad and act according to the principle of godliness that is in him, act according to the power and intelligence and enlightenment of God, that he possesses, and not that he should be watched continually, and be controlled, and act as a slave in these matters. (Lorenzo Snow, *The Teachings of Lorenzo Snow*, ed. Clyde J. Williams [1984], 4)

Our Choices Determine Our Destiny

Our Christian duties are like keys on a piano keyboard: touch them correctly and in concert and renewing music is inevitable; if one chord doesn't lift us, another will! But one must do the touching himself, for we are not dealing with a player piano. (Neal A. Maxwell, *Notwithstanding My Weakness* [1981], 114)

The truly converted will not be diverted from their duties to God or to each other. (Neal A. Maxwell, *If Thou Endure It Well* [1996], 89)

Agency Allows Freedom with Accountability

The gospel can prosper only in an atmosphere of freedom. This fact is confirmed by history, as well as by sacred scriptures. The right of choice—free agency—runs like a golden thread throughout the gospel plan of the Lord for the blessing of His children. (Ezra Taft Benson, *The Teachings of Ezra Taft Benson* [1988], 81)

I should like to suggest three standards by which to judge each of the decisions that determine the behavior patterns of your lives. These standards are so simple as to appear elementary, but I believe their faithful observance will provide a set of moral imperatives by which to govern without argument or equivocation each of our actions and which will bring unmatched rewards. They are:

1. Does it enrich the mind?
2. Does it discipline and strengthen the body?
3. Does it nourish the spirit? (Gordon B. Hinckley, "Caesar, Circus, or Christ?" in *Speeches of the Year, 1965* [2017], 4)

You Are a Disciple of Jesus Christ

Behold, I am a disciple of Jesus Christ, the Son of God. I have been called of him to declare his word among his people, that they might have everlasting life. (3 Nephi 5:13)

A new commandment I give unto you, That ye love one another; as I have loved you, that ye also love one another. By this shall all men know that ye are my disciples, if ye have love one to another. (John 13:34)

He that receiveth my law and doeth it, the same is my disciple; and he that saith he receiveth it and doeth it not, the same is not my disciple, and shall be cast out from among you. (D&C 41:5)

True Discipleship

Heavenly power can be accessed only by those who are Christlike; it is a power whose continued availability is maintained by meekness along with the other virtues. Nor can we have the loving empathy or understanding mercy necessary for true discipleship without meekness. (Neal A. Maxwell, *Meek and Lowly* [1987], 85)

Discipleship is not simply surviving and enduring; discipleship is a pressing forward, a creative Christianity. Discipleship does not wait to be acted upon, but instead acts upon men and circumstances to make things better. . . .

True discipleship is for volunteers only. Only volunteers will trust the Guide sufficiently to follow Him in the dangerous ascent which only He can lead. (*The Neal A. Maxwell Quote Book*, ed. Cory H. Maxwell [1997], 91–92)

Joy in the Success of Others

That is the kind of support I am referring to. When you reach the point where you can enjoy and rejoice in the success of your companion, even when that success exceeds your own, then you have got the real missionary spirit, the real unselfish spirit of love, the spirit of the gospel. When you can rejoice in the success of your companion, then you have a spirit that will make you effective as a missionary. Then you will really be truly, truly happy. Then you will have lost yourself in the service of this wonderful gospel, in service to our Father's children—the greatest work in all the world. (Ezra Taft Benson, *The Teachings of Ezra Taft Benson* [1988], 203)

Missionary Success

The whole secret of our success as far as making converts is concerned is, that we preach the same gospel in all its simplicity and plainness that Jesus preached, and that the Holy Ghost rests upon those who receive it, filling their hearts with joy and gladness unspeakable, and making them as one; and they then know of the doctrine for themselves whether it be of God or man. (Wilford Woodruff, in *Journal of Discourses*, 23:130)

The Test of Discipleship

Scriptural tests establishing true discipleship include: 1. Believing the true doctrines of Christ (Ether 4:10–12); 2. Obeying the principles of the gospel (John 8:31); 3. Having "love one to another" (John 13:35); 4. Accepting the message and aiding the work of the missionaries (D&C 84:87–91); and 5. Bringing forth works of righteousness (John 15:4–8). (Bruce R. McConkie, *Mormon Doctrine*, 2nd ed. [1966], 198)

Herein is my Father glorified, that ye bear much fruit; so shall ye be my disciples. (John 15:8)

Ye are my disciples; and ye are a light unto this people, who are a remnant of the house of Joseph. (3 Nephi 15:12)

Sustaining Our Leaders

She [my mother] always taught us to sustain our bishop and our stake president and the General Authorities. She said that if we did not sustain our leaders, we were not sustaining our God, because they are the representatives of the Lord. She also taught us that when we criticize the leaders of the Church, we are on the road to apostasy. I have tried to follow my mother's teachings in this regard. (James E. Faust, *To Reach Even unto You* [1990], 65)

Follow the Prophet

As I have pondered the messages of the conference, I have asked myself this question: How can I help others partake of the goodness and blessings of our Heavenly Father? The answer lies in following the direction received from those we sustain as prophets, seers, and revelators, and others of the General Authorities. Let us study their words, spoken under the spirit of inspiration, and refer to them often. The Lord has revealed his will to the Saints in this conference. (Howard W. Hunter, *The Teachings of Howard W. Hunter*, ed. Clyde J. Williams [1997], 213)

Follow the Prophet

It is exceedingly important for members of the Church to get experience following the prophets in little things, so that they can follow in large matters. By following the prophets in fair weather we become familiar with their cadence, so that we can follow them in stormy times too, for then both our reflexes and our experience will need to combine to help us; the stresses will be so very real. (Neal A. Maxwell, *All These Things Shall Give Thee Experience* [1979], 102)

The Savior has declared that whether we receive the word of God "by [his] own voice or by the voice of [his] servants, it is the same" (D&C 1:38). If we are to follow Christ, we must follow the prophet, the Lord's mouthpiece on earth. (Joseph B. Wirthlin, *Finding Peace in Our Lives* [1995], 234)

Obedience Is the First Law of Heaven

There is a law, irrevocably decreed in heaven before the foundations of this world, upon which all blessings are predicated—

And when we obtain any blessing from God, it is by obedience to that law upon which it is predicated. (D&C 130:20–21)

That they are willing to take upon them the name of thy Son, and always remember him and keep his commandments which he has given them; that they may always have his Spirit to be with them. Amen. (D&C 20:77)

If ye love me, keep my commandments. . . .

He that hath my commandments, and keepeth them, he it is that loveth me: and he that loveth me shall be loved of my Father, and I will love him, and will manifest myself to him. (John 14:15, 21)

The Prophets Encourages Us to Obey

Obedience must always precede knowledge. You will remember when Adam was driven from the Garden of Eden he offered sacrifices. "An angel of the Lord appeared unto Adam, saying: Why dost thou offer sacrifices unto the Lord? And Adam said unto him: I know not, save the Lord commanded me" (Moses 5:6). Then the angel explained to him the meaning of sacrifices. Obedience must always precede knowledge. If we are obedient to our assigned responsibility, knowledge will follow. We are prone to discount things we cannot understand. (Howard W. Hunter, *The Teachings of Howard W. Hunter*, ed. Clyde J. Williams [1997], 22)

The way to perfection is through obedience. Therefore, to each person is given a pattern—obedience through suffering, and perfection through obedience. Let each person learn obedience of faith in all things and thus exemplify the attributes of the Master. (Spencer W. Kimball, *The Teachings of Spencer W. Kimball*, ed. Edward L. Kimball [1982], 168)

Follow the Prophet with Exactness

Behold ye are worse than they; for as the Lord liveth, if a prophet come among you and declareth unto you the word of the Lord, which testifieth of your sins and iniquities, ye are angry with him, and cast him out. (Helaman 13:26)

I thought how true, and how serious when we begin to choose which of the covenants, which of the commandments we will keep and follow. When we decide that there are some of them that we will not keep or follow, we are taking the law of the Lord into our own hands and become our own prophets, and believe me, we will be led astray, because we are false prophets to ourselves when we do not follow the Prophet of God. No, we should never discriminate between these commandments, as to those we should and should not keep. (N. Eldon Tanner, in Conference Report, Oct. 1966, 98)

Open Your Mouth

In the thirty-third section of the Doctrine and Covenants, the Lord commands us three times in three verses to "open our mouths". . . .

In verse 23, he explains that one of the reasons he called Joseph Smith to his prophetic work was so that "the fullness of [the] gospel might be proclaimed by the weak and the simple unto the ends of the world, and before kings and rulers."

Each of us has the sacred responsibility to proclaim the gospel. The Savior's commandment applies to all members of the Church, not just to full-time missionaries or to returned missionaries. We each have the responsibility to follow the Spirit when it prompts us to share the gospel so that others can come to follow the Savior. (Joseph B. Wirthlin, *Finding Peace in Our Lives* [1995], 240–41)

Missionaries Should Be Bold and Self-Sacrificing

When I read Church history, I am amazed at the boldness of the early brethren as they went out into the world. They seemed to find a way. Even in persecution and hardship, they went and opened doors. . . .

I remember that these fearless men were teaching the gospel in Indian lands before the Church was even fully organized. As early as 1837 the Twelve were in England fighting Satan, in Tahiti in 1844, Australia in 1851, Iceland 1853, Italy 1850, and also in Switzerland Germany, Tonga, Turkey, Mexico, Japan, Czechoslovakia, China, Samoa, New Zealand, South America, France, and Hawaii in 1850. . . .

We must begin to think about our obligation rather than our convenience. The time, I think, has come when sacrifice must be an important element again in the Church. (Spencer W. Kimball, *The Teachings of Spencer W. Kimball*, ed. Edward L. Kimball [1982], 571–72)

To Find People to Teach You Must Open Your Mouth

Open your mouths and they shall be filled, and you shall become even as Nephi of old, who journeyed from Jerusalem in the wilderness.

Yea, open your mouths and spare not, and you shall be laden with sheaves upon your backs, for lo, I am with you.

Yea, open your mouths and they shall be filled, saying: Repent, repent, and prepare ye the way of the Lord, and make his paths straight; for the kingdom of heaven is at hand;

Yea, repent and be baptized, every one of you, for a remission of your sins; yea, be baptized even by water, and then cometh the baptism of fire and of the Holy Ghost. (D&C 33:8–11)

You Are Always Finding

And at all times, and in all places, he shall open his mouth and declare my gospel as with the voice of a trump, both day and night. And I will give unto him strength such as is not known among men. (D&C 24:12)

And we have entered into their houses and taught them, and we have taught them in their streets; yea, and we have taught them upon their hills; and we have also entered into their temples and their synagogues and taught them. (Alma 26:29)

Yea, you shall ever open your mouth in my cause, not fearing what man can do, for I am with you. Amen. (D&C 30:11)

Missionary Work Benefits from Enthusiasm

With such a noble work one should not find it too difficult to develop enthusiasm. Enthusiasm is real interest plus dedicated energy, and this combination provides the most dynamic of all human qualities. But anyone who does not have it naturally can cultivate it by applying autosuggestion. Merely deciding that a job is going to be interesting helps to make it so. . . .

Be positive and enthusiastic. You can be positive without being enthusiastic. Enthusiasm is an effective tool. If your voice is a monotone, train it and give it variety. Let your voice be flexible. You can improve your personalities, you can all improve your voices. (Spencer W. Kimball, *The Teachings of Spencer W. Kimball*, ed. Edward L. Kimball [1982], 573)

The Lord Is Displeased If We Do Not Open Our Mouths

But with some I am not well pleased, for they will not open their mouths, but they hide the talent which I have given unto them, because of the fear of man. Wo unto such, for mine anger is kindled against them.

And it shall come to pass, if they are not more faithful unto me, it shall be taken away, even that which they have. (D&C 60:2–3)

And thou must open thy mouth at all times, declaring my gospel with the sound of rejoicing. Amen. (D&C 28:16)

It is necessary and expedient in me that you should open your mouths in proclaiming my gospel, the things of the kingdom, expounding the mysteries thereof out of the scriptures, according to that portion of Spirit and power which shall be given unto you, even as I will. (D&C 71:1)

Fear Is a Hindrance to Missionary Work

Why should we fear any person in the world when we have such a great thing to give them? But it has been fear that has prevented missionaries from doing their best in the field, and you felt this when you first went out. Fear is engendered by the adversary, and when we once cast aside fear and find what our potential is, that means there's just no limitation. (Howard W. Hunter, *The Teachings of Howard W. Hunter* [1997], 254)

Conquering Fear

I tell you these things because of your prayers; wherefore, treasure up wisdom in your bosoms, lest the wickedness of men reveal these things unto you by their wickedness, in a manner which shall speak in your ears with a voice louder than that which shall shake the earth; but if ye are prepared ye shall not fear. (D&C 38:30)

Wherefore I put thee in remembrance that thou stir up the gift of God, which is in thee by the putting on of my hands.

For God hath not given us the spirit of fear; but of power, and of love, and of a sound mind. (2 Timothy 1:6–7)

There is no fear in love; but perfect love casteth out fear: because fear hath torment. He that feareth is not made perfect in love. (1 John 4:18)

Empowered from on High

Do not be discouraged on account of the greatness of the work; only be humble and faithful. . . . He who scattered Israel has promised to gather them; therefore inasmuch as you are to be instrumental in this great work, He will endow you with power, wisdom, might, and intelligence, and every qualification necessary; while your minds will expand wider and wider, until you can circumscribe the earth and the heavens, reach forth into eternity, and contemplate the mighty acts of Jehovah in all their variety and glory. (Joseph Smith, in *History of the Church*, 4:128–29)

The Word of God Has Power

The Book of Mormon records one of the great lessons from the Nephite experience in these words: "The preaching of the word had a great tendency to lead people to do that which was just, yea, it had a more powerful effect upon the minds of the people than the sword or anything else which had happened to them." (Alma 31:5) When this Book of Mormon prophet, Alma, wrote those words his people were sorely troubled, but his preaching brought about a great reformation which restored peace and happiness. It is so today. This is why we emphasize missionary work as we do. It is the real answer to the world's problems. (Ezra Taft Benson, *The Teachings of Ezra Taft Benson* [1988], 185)

The Strength of Your Message

The scriptures testify of God and contain the words of eternal life. They become the strength of the missionary's message—even the tools of his trade. His confidence will be directly related to his knowledge of God's word. Oh, yes, there are some missionaries who are lazy, less than effective, and anxious for their missions to conclude. A careful examination of such instances will reveal that the actual culprit is not laziness nor disinterest, but is the foe known as *fear.* Our Father chastised such: "With some I am not well pleased, for they will not open their mouths, but they hide the talent which I have given unto them, because of the *fear* of man." (D&C 60:2; italics added) (Thomas S. Monson, *Pathways to Perfection* [1973], 97–98).

The Holy Ghost Converts, Not Missionary Persuasion

Our role as missionaries is not primarily to convince people of the truthfulness of the gospel. If the Lord were primarily interested in convincing people of the divine nature of this work, he could, and perhaps would, demonstrate his powers in such a way that large numbers of people could know the truth in a relatively brief period of time. He could speak if he chose, and all the people on earth could hear in their own language. Or he could emblazon his words in the sky, where all could read or see them. But if those persons thus convinced did not really change their lives for the better, repent of their sins and turn to him in righteousness, they would be worse off than before and would be more insensitive to the whisperings of the Holy Spirit.

No, the Lord is not primarily interested in having his children only convinced of his work. He would like them to be converted to the gospel. (Spencer W. Kimball, *The Teachings of Spencer W. Kimball*, ed. Edward L. Kimball [1982], 569–70)

Humility Is Essential in Missionary Work

To convince people of the divinity of the work one must of necessity be humble. To be arrogant or "cocky" is to threaten to drive away the Holy Ghost who alone can convince and bring testimonies.

Sometimes missionaries boast about the number of conversions they have made. It is the Holy Ghost who convinces men and bears witness to them of the truth of the gospel. Elders might properly tell how many baptisms they performed, for that is physical; but never would it be appropriate for one to claim to himself the conversion of others. (Spencer W. Kimball, *The Teachings of Spencer W. Kimball*, ed. Edward L. Kimball [1982], 569)

Missionary Success Depends on Your Level of Spirituality

Our assignment as missionaries is to plant faith and testimony in the hearts of other people. Some of you will be greatly successful and I will tell you why. You have been set apart as a personal representative of the Lord to teach his children in the mission field. I don't know of a higher calling that could come to any person. You are set apart from all worldly things, worldly influences and thoughts, to a higher plateau—a spiritual plateau where you can live, think, act, and portray the gospel to others. When you can do this and leave all worldly influences behind and live on the new higher plateau, you will be successful. (Howard W. Hunter, *The Teachings of Howard W. Hunter* [1997], 250)

Love Your Investigators

You will not be an effective missionary until you learn to have sympathy for all of our Father's children—unless you learn to love them. People can feel when love is extended to them. Many yearn for it. When you sympathize with their feelings, they in turn will reciprocate goodwill to you. You will have made a friend. And as the Prophet Joseph Smith taught, "Whom can I preach to but my friends." Yes, love the people. (Ezra Taft Benson, *The Teachings of Ezra Taft Benson* [1988], 206)

That Your Fruit Might Remain

There are many living among us everywhere who need that which we have to offer. We have the gospel message, which is entrusted to this church, as the Master said, to go into all the world and preach the gospel to every nation, kindred, tongue, and people (see D&C 133:37). There is no question but that many are being converted in great numbers within the stakes and missions in the Church, but we must always have clear in our minds that we are not out just to make records of the number of baptisms. Our success will be measured not by how many baptisms we have made, but by how many we have brought into the Church who are now becoming active and faithful Church members. (Harold B. Lee, *The Teachings of Harold B. Lee*, ed. Clyde J. Williams [1996], 589)

We Should Be Grateful for the Opportunity to Teach the Gospel

There has never been a period in the history of the Church when missionaries were not called and set apart to fulfill missions somewhere in the world. Each one of us who is here today has been introduced to the Church directly or indirectly through the efforts of some humble missionary. We should be grateful for this—for the part our forefathers played in it and for the opportunity we have today in teaching the gospel to others.

A great opportunity is ours to pass on to others the message of the gospel which has come into our lives. . . . We feel real joy and pleasure when we have the privilege of giving to someone else. . . . Great is the joy and satisfaction of the person who first gave them an understanding of the gospel. Many opportunities are ours, each day we live, to spread the Gospel of Jesus Christ. (Howard W. Hunter, *The Teachings of Howard W. Hunter* [1997], 247)

Teaching the Gospel Is More Important Than Other Good Deeds

You are in the greatest work in the world, and nothing in this world can compare to it. Building homes and bridges is nothing. Building worlds is nothing compared to the lives you are building. The saving of mortal lives isn't any important accomplishment as compared to what you are doing. You might go out here to one of these cemeteries and raise the dead, even a thousand or ten thousand of them, and you haven't done anything compared to what you are doing when you are saving people.

You may heal the sick, the blind may see by the power that you hold, but I want to say, brothers and sisters, you have done little in restoring sight to the blind as compared to that which you do when you bring the light of the gospel to the blind spiritually. (Spencer W. Kimball, *The Teachings of Spencer W. Kimball*, ed. Edward L. Kimball [1982], 547)

Keeping Mission Rules Is a Protection

Any mission president will tell you that whenever a missionary begins to break the rules of the mission, no matter how inconsequential they may seem at the moment, the whole avenue opens up for him to go quickly into other things, and he loses the protection that otherwise would be his. If we would avoid the pitfalls that the ruler of darkness has dug for us, we must put on the whole armor, not just a part of the armor.

We must "put on the whole armour of God" in order to be able "to withstand in the evil day." (Ephesians 6:11, 13) (Harold B. Lee, *The Teachings of Harold B. Lee*, ed. Clyde J. Williams [1996], 596)

Avoiding Discouragement

You must not allow yourselves to become discouraged. Missionary work brings joy, optimism, and happiness. Don't give Satan an opportunity to discourage you. Here again, work is the answer. The Lord has given us a key by which we can overcome discouragement: "Come unto me, all ye that labour and are heavy laden, and I will give you rest. Take my yoke upon you, and learn of me; for I am meek and lowly in heart; and ye shall find rest unto your souls. For my yoke is easy and my burden is light." (Matthew 11:28–30) (Ezra Taft Benson, *The Teachings of Ezra Taft Benson* [1988], 205–6)

To Be Successful, Missionaries Must Avoid Worldly Things

Remember that you have a relatively short time to serve the Lord full-time, and the rest of your life to think about it.

You can't be a part of worldly things and also carry out your role as a representative of the Lord. The two are not compatible. Your objective has been clearly defined for you. From the day you were set apart, you were charged to not be of the world, meaning that you were transferred then from worldly things into a spiritual climate for the duration of your mission. If you have found yourself in this new climate, you are on your way. If you haven't, then you've got some work to do. Satan is always present and will do everything he can to hinder and block and defeat. We encourage you as companionships to help each other in this matter. Two persons dedicated, living in faith, and being prayerful can be an awesome force in the work of the Lord. (Howard W. Hunter, *The Teachings of Howard W. Hunter* [1997], 251–52)

Our Devotion to Serve

We had a missionary in our mission who was particularly devoted and obedient. I said to him one time, "Elder, what is the source of your motivation?"

"Brother Monson," he replied, "I slept in one morning. As I did so, my mind turned to thoughts of my mother and my father, who are operating a little cleaning establishment, working around the clock to earn sufficient money to support me on a mission. As I thought of my parents performing that strenuous work in my behalf, all signs of laziness left me; and I determined that I had an opportunity to serve the Lord in my behalf and in behalf of my own mother and my own father."

Harry Emerson Fosdick said: "Until willingness overflows obligation, men fight as conscripts rather than following the flag as patriots. Duty is never worthily performed until it is performed by one who would gladly do more, if only he could."

In short, we need to extend ourselves in service to our Heavenly Father if we are to demonstrate our love for Him. (Thomas S. Monson, *Live the Good Life* [1988], 107)

The Power of Love

"We increase our love for our Heavenly Father and demonstrate that love by aligning our thoughts and actions with God's word. His pure love directs and encourages us to become more pure and holy. It inspires us to walk in righteousness—not out of fear or obligation but out of an earnest desire to become even more like Him because we love Him"

(Dieter F. Uchtdorf, "The Love of God," *Ensign*, November 2009).

Seek one another's welfare, as the scripture says: "Be kindly affectionate one to another with brotherly love; in honour preferring one another." [See Romans 12:10.] You say that is rather hard; well, but you had better do it. We are told to love our neighbor as ourselves. If we can do this, and then prefer our neighbors to ourselves, and if there is a little advantage, put it on their side, we not only fulfil the law and the prophets, but the gospel. Let us cultivate the spirit of love and kindness, and let every little unpleasantness be buried. (John Taylor, *Deseret News: Semi-Weekly*, Apr. 8, 1879, 1)

Obedience Rules

So much more can be achieved when there is overlapping obedience, as in the case of Abraham and Isaac. A few tasks in the Church are solitary, but most often—whether in a missionary companionship, work on a welfare farm, or a family genealogical organization—overlapping obedience gives a greater impact. If we knew how often the obedience of others is affected by our own and how often our stepping forth soon brings forth a whole platoon of helpers and how often our speaking forth soon creates a chorus—we would be even more ashamed of our slackness and our silence. (Neal A. Maxwell, *Wherefore, Ye Must Press Forward* [1977], 41)

Faithful Obedience

When men obey commands of a creator, it is not blind obedience. How different is the cowering of a subject to his totalitarian monarch and the dignified, willing obedience one gives to his God. The dictator is ambitious, selfish, and has ulterior motives. God's every command is righteous, every directive purposeful, and all for the good of the governed. The first may be blind obedience, but the latter is certainly faith obedience. (Spencer W. Kimball, in Conference Report, Oct. 1954, 52)

Obedience is a requirement of heaven and is therefore a principle of the Gospel. [D&C 82:10; 130:20–21.] Are all required to be obedient? Yes, all. What, against their will? O, no, not by any means. There is no power given to man nor means lawful to be used to compel men to obey the will of God, against their wish, except persuasion and good advice, but there is a penalty attached to disobedience which all must suffer who will not obey the obvious truths or laws of heaven. (Joseph F. Smith, in *Journal of Discourses,* 19:193)

Obedience—The First Law of Heaven

Obedience is the first law of God. It is most important that we should be obedient to the word and will of the Lord. It was that which entitled the Son of God to be anointed above His brethren; for He was in all things most perfect and obedient. . . . The Lord is not going to give us everything without our doing something. He requires of us a broken heart, a contrite spirit, and an obedience to the mind and will of the Lord [D&C 59:8; 82:10]." (Francis M. Lyman, in Conference Report, Oct. 1899, 35)

Learn Obedience

There are several ways the Lord has set for us to learn obedience, so we may prove ourselves and merit His approval and blessings here and eternal glory with Him in the worlds to come.

First of all, we have not been left to walk alone. The Lord has clearly revealed His will concerning His children and shown us His plan of redemption. His laws are explicitly recorded in the standard works of the Church. . . . A second way we learn obedience is by following the counsel of living prophets and other appointed Church leaders. . . . Third, we learn obedience by disciplining our lives in all things. One process by which we discipline ourselves is by repentance. . . .Finally, we learn obedience, as the Savior did, by the things which we suffer. . . .Keeping the commandments of God is not a difficult burden when we do it out of love of Him who has so graciously blessed us. . . . Our willingness to comply with the commandments of God is a witness of our faith in Him and our love for Him. (Delbert L. Stapley, "The Blessings of Righteous Obedience, *Ensign*, Nov. 1977, 18–21)

Missionary Work Is One Way to Take upon Us the Savior's Name

We are to stand as witnesses of God at all times in all places, even until death [Mosiah 18:8–9]. We renew that covenant during the sacrament when we covenant to take the name of Christ upon us.

Missionary service is one important way we take upon ourselves his name. The Savior has said if we desire to take upon us his name, with full purpose of heart, we are called to go into all the world and preach his gospel to every creature (see D&C 18:28).

Those of us who have partaken of the Atonement are under obligation to bear faithful testimony of our Lord and Savior. For he hath said, "I will forgive you of your sins with this commandment—that you remain steadfast in your minds in the solemnity and the spirit of prayer, in bearing testimony to all the world of those things which are communicated unto you." (D&C 84:61) (Howard W. Hunter, *The Teachings of Howard W. Hunter* [1997], 249)

Missionary Work

If you want to keep the Spirit, to love your mission and not be homesick, you must work. But, remember the words of President Thomas S. Monson: "Work without vision is drudgery. Vision without work is dreaming. Work coupled with vision is destiny." There is no greater exhilaration or satisfaction than to know, after a hard day of missionary work, that you have done your best. (Ezra Taft Benson, *The Teachings of Ezra Taft Benson* [1988], 200–1)

The Shield of Faith

To help us be aggressive in our fight [against evil] we do what Paul suggested: "Above all, taking the shield of faith, wherewith ye shall be able to quench all the fiery darts of the wicked. And take the sword of the Spirit, which is the word of God" (Ephesians 6:16–17). Note how the "shield of faith" and the "sword of the Spirit, which is the word of God," work together. Guided by faith taught by the word of God, we view life as a great process of soul training. By faith, as the word of God teaches, we understand that whatever contributes to our becoming more like Him is good for us, even though painful to us at times." (Harold B. Lee, *The Teachings of Harold B. Lee*, ed. Clyde J. Williams [1996], 171)

Guidance of the Holy Spirit

Seek the guidance of the Holy Spirit. Seek it by faith and by prayer, by study, and by righteous living. Learn what the scriptures and the teachings of the Prophet Joseph Smith say about it. Develop a desire for it. Live worthy of it and cultivate its companionship. Take it for your guide. If you do so, your rewards will be eternal; for when the Savior comes in his glory and the parable of the ten virgins is fulfilled—"they that are wise and have received the truth, and have taken the Holy Spirit for their guide, and have not been deceived . . . shall not be hewn down and cast into the fire, but shall abide the day" [D&C 45:57]. (Marion G. Romney, *Learning for the Eternities* [1977], 126)

Alive in Christ Because of Our Faith

In what finally turn out to be the "live with" situations, it is only as one's importuning ends that his "live with" can really begin. This is part of becoming "alive in Christ because of our faith" (2 Nephi 25:25–26). It is only in daily life that we become "dead indeed unto sin" by becoming "alive unto God through Jesus Christ our Lord" (Romans 6:11). No wonder that, reinforcingly and repeatedly, we are counseled to talk of, rejoice in, preach of, and prophecy of Christ. Why? So that we and "our children may know to what source they may look for a remission of their sins" (see 2 Nephi 25:26). Remission brings justified hope, which thereafter companies with faith and charity. Looking to Christ—including looking to His atonement and character—requires our talking and rejoicing over these realities. (Neal A. Maxwell, *Lord, Increase Our faith* [1994], 111)

Accept the Grace of God and Receive Everlasting Life

In ways we cannot comprehend, our sicknesses and infirmities were borne by Him even before they were borne by us. The very weight of our combined sins caused Him to descend below all. We have never been, nor will we be, in depths such as He has known. Thus His atonement made perfect His empathy and His mercy and His capacity to succor us, for which we can be everlastingly grateful as He tutors us in our trials. (Neal A. Maxwell, *Even As I Am* [1982], 116)

The Meek and Lowly Are Full of Faith

Those who are proud of mind demand extrinsic evidence. The Lord told the Prophet Joseph Smith, "Behold, if they will not believe my words, they would not believe you, my servant Joseph, if it were possible that you should show them all these things which I have committed unto you" (D&C 5:7).

On the other hand, those who are humble and meek seek, by faith, to understand truth. They are comfortable with intrinsic as well as extrinsic evidence. They know that "faith is the substance of things hoped for, the evidence of things not seen." (Hebrews 11:1) (Neal A. Maxwell, *Meek and Lowly* [1987], 48)

Faith, Hope, and Charity

And see that ye have faith, hope, and charity, and then ye will always abound in good works. (Alma 7:24)

As I read and ponder the scriptures, I see that developing faith, hope, and charity within ourselves is a step-by-step process. Faith begets hope, and together they foster charity. We read in Moroni, "Wherefore, there must be faith; and if there must be faith there must also be hope; and if there must be hope there must also be charity. These three virtues may be sequential initially, but once obtained, they become interdependent. Each one is incomplete without the others. They support and reinforce each other. Moroni explained, "And except ye have charity ye can in nowise be saved in the kingdom of God; neither can ye be saved in the kingdom of

God if ye have not faith; neither can ye if ye have no hope." (Joseph B. Wirthlin, "Cultivating Divine Attributes," *Ensign*, Nov. 1998, 25)

The Pure Love of Christ

The greater definition of "the pure love of Christ," however, is not what we as Christians try but largely fail to demonstrate toward others but rather what Christ totally succeeded in demonstrating toward us. *True* charity has been known only once. It is shown perfectly and purely in Christ's unfailing, ultimate, and atoning love for us. It is Christ's love for us that "suffereth long, and is kind, and envieth not." It is his love for us that is not "puffed up . . . , not easily provoked, thinketh no evil." It is Christ's love for us that "beareth all things, believeth all things, hopeth all things, endureth all things." It is as demonstrated in Christ that "charity never faileth." It is that charity—his pure love for us—without which we would be nothing, hopeless, of all men and women most miserable. Truly, those found possessed of the blessings of his love at the last day—the Atonement, the Resurrection, eternal life, eternal promise—surely it shall be well with them. (Jeffrey R. Holland, *Christ and the New Covenant: The Messianic Message of the Book of Mormon* [1997], 336)

The Tree of Life

And charity suffereth long, and is kind, and envieth not, and is not puffed up, seeketh not her own, is not easily provoked, thinketh no evil, and rejoiceth not in iniquity but rejoiceth in the truth, beareth all things, believeth all things, hopeth all things, endureth all things.
(Moroni 7:45)

To partake fully of the tree of life is thus to be given the nature of Christ. Those so blessed as to receive this bestowal of the Savior's own character and attributes are filled with charity, because charity is central to the divine nature. The totality of the blessing, however, is complete, sanctified perfection: "Yea, come unto Christ, and be perfected in him. . . . then are ye sanctified in Christ by the grace of God." (Moroni 10:32–33) (Bruce C. Hafen, *The Broken Heart: Applying the Atonement to Life's Experiences* [1989], 196)

The Power of the Book of Mormon

The Book of Mormon is the great standard we are to use in our missionary work. It shows that Joseph Smith was a prophet. It contains the words of Christ, and its great mission is to bring men to Christ. All other things are secondary. The golden question of the Book of Mormon is "Do you want to learn more of Christ?" The Book of Mormon is the great finder of the golden contact. It does not contain things which are "pleasing unto the world," and so the worldly are not interested in it. It is a great sieve. (See 1 Nephi 6:5) (Ezra Taft Benson, *The Teachings of Ezra Taft Benson* [1988], 203)

The Standard of Truth

Our missionaries are going forth in different nations. . . . The standard of truth has been erected; no unhallowed hand can stop the work from progressing; persecutions may rage, mobs may combine, armies may assemble, calumny may defame, but the truth of God will go forth boldly, nobly, and independent, till it has penetrated every continent, visited every clime, swept every country, and sounded in every ear, till the purposes of God shall be accomplished, and the Great Jehovah shall say the work is done. (Joseph Smith, "The Wentworth Letter," *Ensign*, July 2002)

Spiritual Gifts for the Faithful

Miracles and spiritual gifts always attend the faithful. Signs always follow those who believe the true gospel. The fruits of faith always grow on the tree of faith. Whenever the Lord has a people on earth, he endows them with power from on high. The presence of miracles, signs, wonders, and gifts of the Spirit stands as conclusive proof of the divine commission of those whom the Lord has called to minister in his place and stead among the children of men. (Bruce R. McConkie, *A New Witness for the Articles of Faith* [1985], 363)

Faith in Jesus Christ

Now let me describe to you what faith in Jesus Christ means. Faith in Him is more than mere acknowledgment that He lives. It is more than professing belief. Faith in Jesus Christ consists of complete reliance on Him. As God, He has infinite power, intelligence, and love. There is no human problem beyond His capacity to solve. Because He descended below all things, He knows how to help us rise above our daily difficulties. (Ezra Taft Benson, *The Teachings of Ezra Taft Benson* [1988], 66)

A Wise Steward

"And whoso is found a faithful, a just, and a wise steward shall enter into the joy of his Lord, and shall inherit eternal life" (D&C 51:19). Those words intrigue me. "A faithful, a just, and a wise steward." Every man here has a stewardship for others—faithful, just, and wise. Faithful in all he is asked to do. Just, even-handed, considerate of all for whom he has responsibility. Wise, with that wisdom which comes from the Lord. I would like to suggest that one verse to you as something you could write out and put on the mirror so that every morning you will see it and think of it and ponder it in terms of your responsibility. (Gordon B. Hinckley, *Teachings of Gordon B. Hinckley* [1997], 613)

Take Up Your Cross

We save our lives by losing them for His sake. As you find yourself, you will find God. This is true. I declare that to you. It is His promise. Take up the real cross of Jesus Christ.

What kind of cross do you bear? What is its shape, weight, size, or dimension? We all have them. Some are very visible, while others are not always evident. Sometimes the heaviest personal cross could be to carry no cross at all. Some crosses we bear are these (maybe you will relate to one or more): the cross of loneliness; the cross of physical limitations—the loss of a leg, an arm, hearing, seeing, mobility—obvious crosses (we see people with these crosses and admire their strength in carrying them with dignity); the cross of poor health; the cross of transgression; the cross of success; the cross of temptation; the cross of beauty, fame, or wealth; the cross of financial burdens; the cross of criticism; the cross of peer rejection. (Marvin J. Ashton, *Be of Good Cheer* [1987], 32)

We Should Be Diligent in God's Service

Having received the light of the everlasting gospel, and partaken of the good things of the kingdom, and being of the seed of Israel and heirs to great and glorious promises, we should labor with fidelity and diligence to accomplish what God has designed to do through us. We should be men and women of faith and power as well as good works; and when we discover ourselves careless or indifferent in the least, it should be sufficient for us to know it in order to mend our ways and return to the path of duty. . . .

We should renew our covenants before God and the holy angels that we will, God being our helper, serve Him more faithfully during the ensuing year than we have in the past, that our public and private life, our actions and the spirit and influence we wield may be in keeping with the motto, "The Kingdom of God or nothing." (Lorenzo Snow, *The Teachings of Lorenzo Snow*, ed. Clyde J. Williams [1984], 48)

The Gift of the Holy Ghost

The gift of the Holy Ghost . . . quickens all the intellectual faculties, increases, enlarges, expands, and purifies all the natural passions and affections, and adapts them by the gift of wisdom to their lawful use. . . . It inspires virtue, kindness, goodness, tenderness, gentleness and charity. It develops beauty of person, form and features. It tends to health, vigor, animation and social feeling. It develops and invigorates all the faculties of the physical and intellectual man. It strengthens, invigorates, and gives tone to the nerves. In short, it is, as it were, marrow to the bone, joy to the heart, light to the eyes, music to the ears, and life to the whole being. (Parley P. Pratt, *Key to the Science of Theology*, 101–2)

Enlightened by the Holy Spirit

It will come by the Holy Spirit, not by scholarly study or by mortal reasoning. When it comes, it will reveal to those who fear God and serve him "all mysteries, yea, all the hidden mysteries of [God's] kingdom from days of old, and for ages to come" (D&C 76:7). "Yea, verily I say unto you, in that day when the Lord shall come, he shall reveal all things" (D&C 101:32). In that day, as foreseen by Isaiah, "the earth shall be full of the knowledge of the Lord." (Isaiah 11:9; 2 Nephi 21:9; also see D&C 84:98)

Those who receive this revelation are described: "Their wisdom shall be great, and their understanding reach to heaven; and before them the wisdom of the wise shall perish, and the understanding of the prudent shall come to naught. For by my Spirit will I enlighten them, and by my power will I make known unto them the secrets of my will—

yea, even those things which eye has not seen, nor ear heard, nor yet entered into the heart of man." (D&C 76:9–10) (Dallin H. Oaks, *The Lord's Way* [1991], 74)

A Happy Missionary

The busy missionary is the happy missionary. I cannot recall a missionary who was really active and busy ever going astray. Occasionally we have missionaries who make mistakes. It usually starts when they become idle, when they stay in their lodgings when they ought to be out with the people. Occasionally you will find a missionary who is looking for excuses for not going out—who can look out the window and see a storm coming when there isn't any, who can see rain when it isn't raining. The important thing is to get out with the people, to keep active, to be devoted. Do not sleep longer than is needful. . . . So cease from all light-mindedness, cease to sleep longer than is needful, and retire to your bed early (see D&C 88:121, 124). You will be more effective, you will do more work, you will be happier, and you will have better health. (Ezra Taft Benson, *The Teachings of Ezra Taft Benson* [1988], 205)

The Love of God Is the Source of All Happiness

And it came to pass that I beheld a tree, whose fruit was desirable to make one happy. (1 Nephi 8:10)

And it came to pass that I beheld that the rod of iron, which my father had seen, was the word of God, which led to the fountain of living waters, or to the tree of life; which waters are a representation of the love of God; and I also beheld that the tree of life was a representation of the love of God. (1 Nephi 11:25)

Chastisement of the Lord Prepares the Way for Forgiveness

"Verily, thus saith the Lord unto you whom I love, and whom I love I also chasten that their sins may be forgiven, for with the chastisement I prepare a way for their deliverance in all things out of temptation, and I have loved you." (D&C 95:1). . . .

The Lord taught that the chastisement that would prepare them to be forgiven would also produce a shield against temptation.

The broken heart and contrite spirit that are the requirements for forgiveness are also its fruits.

The very humility that is the sign of having been forgiven is protection against future sin. And it is by avoiding future sin that we retain a remission of the sins of the past. (Henry B. Eyring, *To Draw Closer to God: A Collection of Discourses* [1997], 51)

Blessings of the Holy Ghost

The gifts, blessings and power of the Spirit are almost without number. You must seek the best gifts (see Moroni 10:4–25; D & C 46:7–33). You will remember that the Spirit will comfort you, teach you all things, and bring things to your remembrance (see John 14:26). You are sanctified by the Holy Ghost (see Romans 15:16; 3 Nephi 27:20). You can speak and teach by the Spirit (see 2 Peter 1:21; D&C 42:14; 68:3–7). You can be shown all things to do (see 2 Nephi 32:5) and be led not knowing beforehand the things you should do (see 1 Nephi 4:6). Lest you forget, the Holy Ghost will show you the truth of all things (see Moroni 10:5). Remember Paul's advice to Timothy: "Wherefore I put thee in remembrance that thou stir up the gift of God, which is in thee by the putting on of my hands" (2 Timothy 1:6) . . . and that great gift is the gift of the Holy Ghost.

Receiving the Holy Ghost

As with all gifts, this gift must be received and accepted to be enjoyed. When priesthood hands were laid upon your head to confirm you a member of the Church, you heard the words, "Receive the Holy Ghost." This did not mean that the Holy Ghost unconditionally became your constant companion. Scriptures warn us that the Spirit of the Lord will "not always strive with man." When we are confirmed, we are given the *right* to the companionship of the Holy Ghost, but it is a right that we must continue to earn through obedience and worthiness. We cannot take this gift for granted. (Joseph B. Wirthlin, "The Unspeakable Gift," *Ensign*, May 2003, 26)

Things You Learn as a Missionary

A missionary learns that God, our Heavenly Father, can and does answer prayers. He learns to recognize the promptings of the Holy Spirit and to be directed by that Spirit. He prays for his own welfare—to be humble and susceptible to the influence of the Holy Ghost—as well as for the people with whom he is laboring. Through these experiences of prayer and service, he learns to love the Lord with all his heart and to more fully love his fellowmen. (Ezra Taft Benson, *The Teachings of Ezra Taft Benson* [1988], 182)

Scripture Study

Scriptures contain the record of the self-revelation of God, and through them God speaks to man. Where could there be more profitable use of time than reading from the scriptural library, the literature that teaches us to know God and understand our relationship to him? Time is always precious; but study of the scriptures is absolutely essential. . . .

We hope that you are studying the gospel regularly. Read from the scriptures, especially the Book of Mormon, each day as individuals and as families. Study the word of the Lord, and your faith and testimony will increase. What could be a more profitable use of discretionary time than reading from the scriptural library, the literature that teaches us to know God and understand our relationship to him? (Howard W. Hunter, *The Teachings of Howard W. Hunter*, ed. Clyde J. Williams [1997], 50)

Our Faith Can Be Refreshed Every Day

Our faith can be freshened in yet other ways. Those fed at the miracle of the loaves and fishes have long since gone to their reward, as have also the ten lepers. However, the same Lord who fed and healed loves us no less, nor is He less powerful than He was two thousand years ago. How blessed we are to have "proofs" of the longevity of His Lordship! Moreover, His working out of the miracle of the Atonement gives us each everlasting blessings, while the wine produced in the miracle at Cana is long gone. Jesus' blessings, both personal and universal, continue with us to this very day. (Neal A. Maxwell, *Even As I Am* [1982], 7)

Your Calling Is to Bless Others

Now, your responsibility to touch lives might seem overwhelming. You can take heart that you were called by the Savior. . . .

He will make you a fisher of men, however inadequate you may feel now. It won't be done by a mysterious process. It will be the natural result of your choosing to follow him. Just think about what you must do to be a fisher of men, to touch lives with faith for him. You will need to love the people you serve. You will need to be humble and full of hope. You will need to have the Holy Ghost as your companion to know when to speak and what to say and how to testify. (Henry B. Eyring, *To Draw Closer to God: A Collection of Discourses* [1997], 190)

An Instrument in the Hands of the Lord

A missionary learns, for example, that God can use him as an instrument to accomplish His work. He can say, as did Ammon, a Book of Mormon missionary, "This is [a] blessing which hath been bestowed upon us, that we have been made instruments in the hands of God to bring about this great work" (Alma 26:3). A missionary learns that he must be humble and dependent on the Lord. He learns to pray with fervor and sincerity, not only for himself but for others, and to be led and directed by the Spirit. (Ezra Taft Benson, *The Teachings of Ezra Taft Benson* [1988], 182)

Pleasing Heavenly Father Is Your Goal

Missionary responsibility belongs to members in all lands. We want you to know that this is really serious business. We're not merely inviting people to go on missions. We are saying, This is your work! The God of heaven, through his prophets, has called you to this service. (Spencer W. Kimball, *The Teachings of Spencer W. Kimball*, ed. Edward L. Kimball [1982], 549)

Every young man seeking to please his Heavenly Father would be willing and anxious to give approximately a tithe of his life at the age of nineteen or twenty to go into the world to preach the gospel. He would save his money for this; he would plan his life's program around it; he would keep himself physically, mentally, and morally alert, as well as spiritually strong, to be prepared for this great and sacred responsibility. (Gordon B. Hinckley, *Teachings of Gordon B. Hinckley* [1997], 346)

Pray for a Grateful Heart

Cultivate a spirit of thanksgiving for the blessing of life and for the marvelous gifts and privileges each of us enjoy. The Lord has said that the meek shall inherit the earth (see Matthew 5:5). I cannot escape the interpretation that meekness implies a spirit of gratitude as opposed to an attitude of self-sufficiency, an acknowledgment of a greater power beyond oneself, a recognition of God, and an acceptance of his commandments. This is the beginning of wisdom. Walk with gratitude before him who is the giver of life and every good gift. (Gordon B. Hinckley, "With All Thy Getting Get Understanding," *Ensign*, Aug. 1988, 3–4)

Ponder and Pray—Receive Revelation

Therefore, go ye unto your homes, and ponder upon the things which I have said, and ask of the Father, in my name, that ye may understand, and prepare your minds for the morrow, and I come unto you again. (3 Nephi 17:3)

We need the Spirit of the Lord in our lives more. . . . But there is hardly time to reflect and think and pause and meditate. I daresay that most of those in this room today have not taken an hour in the last year to just sit down quietly, each man to himself, as a son of God, reflecting upon his place in this world, upon his destiny, upon his capacity to do good, upon his mission to make some changes for good. We need to. I recall so vividly President McKay in his old age in a meeting with his counselors and the Twelve saying, "Brethren, we need to take more time to meditate, to think quietly." (Gordon B. Hinckley, *Teachings of Gordon B. Hinckley* [1997], 334)

True Disciples Are Meek

Meekness, nevertheless, comes trailing a cloud of other beneficial considerations. The prophet Mormon observed that without meekness, there can be no faith nor hope nor love (Moroni 7:37–47). Furthermore, remission of our sins brings additional meekness along with the great gift of the Holy Ghost, the Comforter (Moroni 8:26). These supernal blessings are not to be enjoyed for any length of time except by those who are meek. But of the joys of the gospel, it has been rightly said, "None receiveth save it be the truly penitent and humble seeker of happiness." (Alma 27:18) (Neal A. Maxwell, *Meek and Lowly* [1987], 84)

Serve in Meekness

Go in all meekness, in sobriety, and preach Jesus Christ and Him crucified; not to contend with others on account of their faith, or systems of religion, but pursue a steady course. This I delivered by way of commandment, and all who observe it not, will pull down persecution upon their heads, while those who do shall always be filled with the Holy Ghost; this I pronounced as a prophecy. (Joseph Smith, *Teachings of the Prophet Joseph Smith*, comp. Joseph Fielding Smith [1938], 109)

Hunger and Thirst after Righteousness

Fundamental to most wrongdoing are a lack of desire, the absence of a strong motive or the right influence, and a deficiency in living the precepts. Individuals who do right and "hunger and thirst after righteousness" (Matthew 5:6) receive and keep alive through their actions the feeling to do right. Inherent in the first principles of the gospel is the "desire principle"—the desire to love God and fellowmen "with all thy heart, and with all thy soul, and with all thy mind" (Matthew 22:37). To attain these heights, each of us must work in harmony with God's will and create a spiritual climate that will bring Jesus into the midst of our lives, and then we must continue to live "with an eye single to [his] glory." (D&C 4:5) (Joseph B. Wirthlin, *Finding Peace in Our Lives* [1995], 98)

Peace through Righteousness and Christ the Lord

No man is at peace with himself or his God who is untrue to his better self, who transgresses the law of right either in dealing with himself by indulging in passion, in appetite, yielding to temptations against his accusing conscience, or in dealing with his fellowmen, being untrue to their trust. Peace does not come to the transgressor of law; peace comes by obedience to law, and it is that message which Jesus would have us proclaim among men. (David O. McKay, in Conference Report, Oct. 1938, 130)

Missionaries Are Pure in Heart

To be "pure in heart" is to achieve that condition in which motives, desires, and attitudes are acceptable to God and consistent with the eternal progress that is the ultimate destiny of his children. . . .

To become pure in heart—to achieve exaltation—we must alter our attitudes and priorities to a condition of spirituality, we must control our thoughts, we must reform our motives, and we must perfect our desires. How can this be done?

The first step in the alteration of our attitudes and our priorities is to face up to our own imperfections and the need to change. . . .

To achieve spirituality and to reform our motives and perfect our desires we must learn to control our thoughts. The prophet Alma taught his faithful son Helaman: "Let all thy thoughts be directed unto the Lord; yea, let the affections of thy heart be placed upon the Lord forever." (Alma 37:36) (Dallin H. Oaks, *Pure in Heart* [1988], 137, 140, 145)

Ye Are the Salt of the Earth

Members of the Church have power to become the salt of the earth, that is "to be the seasoning, savoring, preserving influence in the world, the influence which would bring peace and blessings to all others" (*Mormon Doctrine*, 601). "When men are called unto mine everlasting gospel, and covenant with an everlasting covenant," the Lord says, "they are accounted as the salt of the earth and the savor of men; They are called to be the savor of men; therefore, if that salt of the earth lose its savor, behold, it is thenceforth good for nothing only to be cast out and trodden under the feet of men." (D&C 101:39–40; 103:9–10) (Bruce R. McConkie, *Doctrinal New Testament Commentary*, 3 vols. [1966–73], 1:218)

Let Your Light Shine

The cumulative radiance of our candles, as members of The Church of Jesus Christ of Latter-day Saints, can illuminate a world filled with darkness, leading many others into the glorious light of the gospel. Darkness, after all, is the absence of light.

As our lights glow and illuminate, we must be certain that we are walking in the straight and narrow way prescribed by the Savior. If we fail in this mandate, we might be compared to a lighthouse built in a deceptive location, luring trusting sailors to their watery deaths. We must be certain that our lights are leading in the right direction. We might well ask ourselves, "What will happen in my family, in my community, in my church, if people follow my light?" Or we might ask, "What kind of a world would this world be if everyone were just like me?"

If we are to be a light to the world, we must guard against letting our light flicker or go out. (Joseph B. Wirthlin, *Finding Peace in Our Lives* [1995], 78–79)

Teach by Example

We care for others. At the end of the day, our belief in Christ will best be reflected to others by the extent to which we practice what we preach. Elder Neal A. Maxwell has reminded us: "Overall, the perception of us as a Church and people will improve in direct proportion to the degree to which we mirror the Master in our lives. No media effort can do as much good—over the sweep of time—as can *believing*, *behaving*, and *serving* members of the Church! The eloquence of such examples will be felt and seen in any culture or community. (Alexander B. Morrison, *Feed My Sheep: Leadership Ideas for Latter-day Shepherds* [1992], 134)

Gaining Your Testimony

You must have a burning testimony of the divinity of this work if you are going to succeed. Your first obligation is to get that testimony through prayer, through fasting, through meditation, through study, through appealing to the Lord to give you the testimony, through responding to calls when they come to you. You must have a testimony of the divinity of this work. You must know that God lives; that Jesus is the Christ, the Redeemer of the world; that Joseph Smith is a prophet of God; that the priesthood and authority of our Heavenly Father is here; and that you bear that priesthood and have the authority to represent Him in the world. (Ezra Taft Benson, *The Teachings of Ezra Taft Benson* [1988], 192–93)

Be Prayerful

Be prayerful. You can't do it alone. You know that. You cannot make it alone and do your best. You need the help of the Lord . . . and the marvelous thing is that you have the opportunity to pray, with the expectation that your prayers will be heard and answered. . . . The marvelous thing about prayer is that it is personal, it's individual, it's something that no one else gets into, in terms of your speaking with your Father in Heaven in the name of the Lord Jesus Christ. Be prayerful.

Ask the Lord to forgive your sins. As the Lord for help. Ask the Lord to bless you. Ask the Lord to help you realize your righteous ambitions. . . . Ask the Lord for all of the important things that mean so much to you in your lives. He stands ready to help. Don't ever forget it. (Gordon B. Hinckley, *Teachings of Gordon B. Hinckley* [1997], 468)

Special Counsel for Your Mission

If you go on a mission to preach the Gospel with lightness and frivolity in your hearts, looking for this and that, and to learn what is in the world, and not having your minds riveted—yes, I may say riveted—on the cross of Christ, you will go and return in vain. Go forth weeping, bearing precious seed, full of the power of God, and full of faith to heal the sick even by the touch of your hand, rebuking and casting out foul spirits, and causing the poor among men to rejoice, and you will return bringing your sheaves with you. Let your minds be centered on your missions and labor earnestly to bring souls to Christ. (Brigham Young, *Discourses of Brigham Young*, sel. John A. Widtsoe [1954], 325)

Applying the Atonement to Life

"We believe that through the Atonement of Christ, all mankind may be saved, by obedience to the laws and ordinances of the Gospel" (Third Article of Faith). Salvation does not come to those who merely confess Christ with their lips, or even to those who go about doing good works (as men generally view good works). It is reserved for those who do the very things which constitute the will of the Father, namely: (1) Accept and believe the true gospel, thus gaining faith in Christ, and thus believing in the prophets sent by Christ to reveal his truths, Joseph Smith being the greatest of these in this dispensation; (2) Repent; (3) Be baptized by a legal administrator who has power from God to bind on earth and seal in heaven; (4) Receive the gift of the Holy Ghost, also by the authorized act of a duly appointed priesthood bearer; and (5) Endure in righteousness and devotion to the truth, keeping every standard of personal righteousness that appertains to the gospel, until the end of one's mortal probation. (Bruce R. McConkie, *Doctrinal New Testament Commentary,* 3 vols. [1965–73], 1:254)

Faith Precedes the Miracle

"Dispute not because ye see not," the prophet Moroni says in another passage, "for ye receive no witness until after the trial of your faith" (Ether 12:6). Speaking of this scriptural direction, President Spencer W. Kimball says: "Father Adam understood this basic principle: 'An angel of the Lord appeared unto Adam, saying: why dost thou offer sacrifices unto the Lord? And Adam said unto him: I know not, save the Lord commanded me' (Moses 5:6). . . . Men have often misunderstood and have reversed the process. They would have the harvest before the planting, the reward before the service, the miracle before the faith."

Jesus taught (and his prophets taught after him) that "signs shall follow them that believe" (Mark 16:17; Mormon 9:24; D&C 84:65). The Book of Mormon teaches the principle in these words: "Neither at any time hath any wrought miracles until after their faith; wherefore they first believed in the Son of God." (Ether 12:18) (Dallin H. Oaks, *The Lord's Way* [1991], 83)

Feed Your Faith and Doubt Your Fears

As leaders in Israel, we must seek to dispel fear from among our people. A timid, fearing people cannot do their work well. The Latter-day Saints have a divinely assigned world-mission so great that they cannot afford to dissipate their strength in fear. The Lord has repeatedly warned His people against fear. Many a blessing is withheld because of our fears. He has expressly declared that men cannot stop his work on earth, therefore, they who are engaged in the Lord's latter-day cause and who fear, really trust man more than God, and thereby are robbed of their power to serve. (John A. Widtsoe, in Conference Report, Apr. 1942, 33)

Assist in the Work of Immortality and Eternal Life

God, our Heavenly Father, designs that all who will observe truth and righteousness should possess wisdom and understanding for themselves, and He is bringing us through circumstances that will develop within us that portion of the Godhead or Deity which we have received from Him, that we may become worthy of our high and glorious parentage. This being His design respecting us, we should seek by every means in our power to aid Him in carrying it out, until the whole people are enlightened by His Spirit, and act understandingly and in concert in carrying out His designs. (George Q. Cannon, in *Journal of Discourses*, 12:46–47)

A Marvelous Work and a Wonder

This "marvelous work and a wonder" has come to pass and has spread all over the world where there has been religious liberty; and from every land and from every clime honest, faithful, God-fearing men and women have heard the sound of the true voice of the shepherd through his servants who have gone forth to proclaim the Gospel. And men of great influence have been gathered into this Church. Men like John Taylor, who presided over the Church, heard the Gospel in a foreign land; the parents of George Q. Cannon, and many other leaders in this Church, heard the sound of this Gospel and embraced it and gathered to Zion, and labored with all the power and ability that they possessed for the advancement of God's kingdom. Year by year this great and wonderful work has rolled on and we are becoming known as a God-fearing people, as a people with a destiny that is sure to be fulfilled. (Heber J. Grant, in Conference Report, Oct. 1929, 9)

Let Everyone Hear the Gospel

"The Savior's call is to you of the rising generation. He is asking for worthy, prepared, faithful young men and young women who will heed the prophet's voice, who will step up and say, as the Savior Himself said, 'Here am I, send me' (Abraham 3:27). The need has never been greater. The field has never been whiter. You are called to go 'this last time' (Jacob 5:62). There is no greater work; there is no greater call than teaching 'all nations, baptizing them in the name of the Father, and of the Son, and of the Holy Ghost' (Matthew 28:19)." (Brent H. Nielson, "A Call to the Rising Generation," *Ensign*, Nov. 2009)

Ye Are the Witnesses of Gospel Truths

I come to you with a witness as sure as was the Apostle Paul's, perhaps in a manner in which the Apostle Paul received his. A witness more perfect than sight is the witness by which the Holy Ghost bears witness to one's soul that he knows these things are true. I witness to you tonight, with all my soul, that I know, as the Spirit has borne witness to my soul, that the Savior lives. To you who may not have that testimony, may I ask you to hold to my testimony until you have developed one for yourselves. But work on it, study, and pray until you too can know with a certainty that these things are true—that God lives and this is the plan of salvation. (Harold B. Lee, *The Teachings of Harold B. Lee*, ed. Clyde J. Williams [1996], 640)

Magnify Your Calling

In the Church and kingdom of God there is no unimportant office or calling or service (see 1 Corinthians 12:12–25). We are all in it together; and the Lord has a way of magnifying us. . . .

It is essential to all we do in our ministry that it be done with "an eye single to the glory of God" (D&C 4:5). That should be our primary motive. We have not been called to build up ourselves, but to build the kingdom of God. We shall be instrumental in achieving this momentous goal as we magnify our callings and honor the Lord. (Ezra

Taft Benson, *The Teachings of Ezra Taft Benson* [1988], 453–54)

Receiving Revelation

In its most familiar forms, revelation comes by means of words or thoughts or feelings communicated to the mind. "Behold," the Lord told Oliver Cowdery, "I will tell you in your mind and in your heart, by the Holy Ghost" (D&C 8:2). This is the experience Enos described when he said, "The voice of the Lord came into my mind" (Enos 1:10). It is the experience Nephi described when he reminded his wayward brothers that the Lord had spoken to them in a still small voice, but they "were past feeling" and "could not feel his words" (1 Nephi 17:45).

We often refer to these most familiar forms of revelation as *inspiration.* Inspired thoughts or promptings can take the form of enlightenment of the mind (D&C 6:15), positive or negative feelings about proposed courses of action. . . .

The experience of revelation is available to everyone. President Lorenzo Snow declared that it is "the grand privilege of every Latter-day Saint

. . . to have the manifestations of the spirit every day of our lives." (Dallin H. Oaks, *The Lord's Way* [1991], 23)

You Reap What You Sow

In this world and the universe the student finds constantly increasing evidence of the operation of law; whether it be in stellar space, among the planets, or in the minute revolving universe within the atom, the same law is operating.

I should like to pause long enough to say to you that the most arresting declaration that you can make to the youth of your wards and stakes and missions is that there is a law which applies to them; it is inexorable, immutable; it is known as the law of the harvest. "As ye sow, so shall ye reap." The Lawmaker is not capricious or arbitrary, there are no favorites, no one is exempt. "As ye sow, so shall ye reap." It would be well for you to remind them that in the springtime of life as in the springtime of seasons the soil and the seed determine the harvest and that sowing is an ongoing continuing process. (Hugh B. Brown, *Continuing the Quest* [1961], 176)

You Have a Right to Revelation

Revelation may be given to every member of the Church. The Prophet said that every man should be a prophet; that the testimony of Jesus is the spirit of prophecy. It is not only the privilege but the duty of each member of the Church to know the truth which will make him free. This he cannot know unless it is revealed to him. Moroni has promised every person who humbly and sincerely reads the Book of Mormon that he may know by revelation that it is true. The gift of the Holy Ghost is given to the members of the Church so that they may have the spirit of prophecy and revelation. . . . But the members of the Church are entitled to receive revelation which is needful for their progress, and if they will hearken to the Spirit of truth and walk humbly before the Lord, they will not fall short of this spiritual guidance. (Joseph Fielding Smith, *Church History and Modern Revelation* [1949], 4:36)

Pray Always

Prayer, in fact, is to be a reflection of our attitude toward God and life. In this sense, we can always be praying. (Luke 18:1)

Clearly, however, since praying is a part of living, if we are not living righteously the quality of our prayers will be affected. Likewise, routine personal prayers will scarcely reflect the unevenness of life, especially those moments when we are in deep need. When in deep need, we, as did He, "being in agony" will need to pray "more earnestly" (Luke 22:44). . . .

The Lord's disciples said to him, "Lord, teach us to pray" (Luke 11:1). Jesus then gave a marvelous model of what prayer could be. . . . No single prayer will suffice for all circumstances!

There are no Christlike prayers, however, that do not include, as did the Lord's Prayer, deep expressions of gratitude and appreciation to our Father in heaven along with a submittal to Him. (Neal A. Maxwell, *All These Things Shall Give Thee Experience* [1979], 92–93)

The Spirit of Revelation

There is a way by which persons can keep their consciences clear before God and man, and that is to preserve within them the Spirit of God, which is the spirit of revelation to every man and woman. It will reveal to them, even in the simplest of matters, what they shall do, by making suggestions to them. We should try to learn the nature of this spirit, that we may understand its suggestions, and then we will always be able to do right. This is the grand privilege of every Latter-day Saint. We know that it is our right to have the manifestations of the spirit every day of our lives. . . . From the time we receive the Gospel, go down into the waters of baptism and have hands laid upon us afterwards for the gift of the Holy Ghost, we have a friend, if we do not drive it from us by doing wrong. That friend is the Holy Spirit, the Holy Ghost, which partakes of the things of God and shows them unto us. This is a grand means that the Lord has provided for us, that we may know the light, and not be groveling continually in the dark [D&C 88:66–68]. (Lorenzo Snow, in Conference Report, Apr. 1899, 52)

The Power of Humility

The Lord has said that no one can assist with this work unless he is humble and full of love (see D&C 12:8). But humility does not mean weakness. It does not mean timidity; it does not mean fear. A man can be humble and also fearless. A man can be humble and also courageous. Humility is the recognition of our dependence upon a higher power, a constant need for the Lord's support in His work. . . .

We must develop a love for people. Our hearts must go out to them in the pure love of the gospel, in a desire to lift them, to build them up, to point them to a higher, finer life and eventually to exaltation in the celestial kingdom of God. We emphasize the fine qualities of the people with whom we associate, and love them as children of God whom the Lord loves. (Ezra Taft Benson, *Come unto Christ* [1983], 94–95)

The Blessings of Missionary Work

We are engaged in missionary service to testify of the greatest event that has transpired in this world since the resurrection of the Master: the coming of God the Father and His Son, Jesus Christ, to the boy-prophet, Joseph Smith. We are sent out to testify of a new volume of scripture, a new witness for Christ.

Missionary work provides us the happiest years of our lives. I know whereof I speak. I have tasted the joy of missionary work. There is no work in all the world that can bring an individual greater joy and happiness. Like Ammon of old, our joy can be full because of seeing others come into the kingdom of God. (Ezra Taft Benson, *Come unto Christ* [1983], 95)

Heeding the Words of Our Living Prophets

May each Church member seek to possess the inner spiritual strength which flows from faithfully heeding the words of the living prophets. Such loyalty and obedience will clothe us with the protective armor of God. As we carefully cling to those teachings and testimonies, we will neither be moved by modern anti-Christs nor deceived by the sophistries of the adversary. Just as Arabella Smith would not abandon her duty and let go of the rope despite personal pain and hardship, we too must never "let go" of the living prophets. They will not abandon us; let us not abandon them. "We have been promised that the President of the Church will receive guidance for all of us as the revelator for the Church," Elder James E. Faust taught. "Our safety lies in paying heed to that which he says and following his counsel." (James E. Faust, in Conference Report, Oct. 1989, 11)

Patience—A Divine Attribute

I believe that lack of patience is a major cause of many difficulties and much unhappiness in the world today. Too often we are impatient with ourselves, with our family members and friends, and even with the Lord. . . .

To the Latter-day Saints, the Lord gave patience as one of the divine attributes that qualifies a person for the ministry (see D&C 4:6). He counseled them to be patient in their afflictions (see D&C 24:8; 31:9; 54:10; 98:23–24), and to make their decisions in patience (see D&C 107:30). He taught us to be perfect (see Matthew 5:48; 3 Nephi 12:48) and said, "Ye are not able to abide the presence of God now, neither the ministering of angels; wherefore, continue in patience until ye are perfected" (D&C 67:13).

The Lord Jesus Christ is our perfect example of patience. (Joseph B. Wirthlin, *Finding Peace in Our Lives* [1995], 203)

Missionaries Should Take Initiative and Be Their "Brother's Keeper"

Someone has said that initiative is doing the right thing at the right time without having to be told. What a thrilling thing it is to see an aggressive, resourceful, willing, untiring, well-directed, spiritual . . . missionary who can do the right things on his own initiative and keep on doing them to the end. (Spencer W. Kimball, *The Teachings of Spencer W. Kimball*, ed. Edward L. Kimball [1982], 572)

Missionaries are responsible for companions. Now I ask, nearly every time I interview a missionary, "Suppose you and your companion are in a distant town and he begins to flirt and break all the mission rules, where is your loyalty?" He is puzzled at first. He would like to be true to a fellow missionary. I know what is in his mind. I ask him where is his loyalty, to a lawbreaker or to the kingdom; to a companion who will not yield to the proper rules and regulations, or to your God in heaven? (Spencer W. Kimball, *The Teachings of Spencer W. Kimball*, ed. Edward L. Kimball [1982], 580)

Our Motive Is to Make People Happy

As representatives of the Church we have the responsibility to go among them with love, as servants of the Lord, as representatives of the Master of heaven and earth. They may not altogether appreciate that; they may resent that as being egotistical and unfair, but that would not change my attitude. I am not going to make them unhappy if I can help it. I would like to make them happy, especially when I think of the marvelous opportunities that have come to me because of membership in this blessed church. (George Albert Smith, in Conference Report, Oct. 1945)

The Missionary Spirit

I rejoice in proclaiming this glorious gospel, because it takes root in the hearts of the children of men, and they rejoice with me to be connected with, and participate in, the blessings of the kingdom of God. I rejoice in afflictions, for they are necessary to humble and prove us, that we may comprehend ourselves, become acquainted with our weakness and infirmities; and I rejoice when I triumph over them, because God answers my prayers; therefore I feel to rejoice all the day long. . . .

I, myself, have traveled hundreds of thousands of miles preaching the gospel; and without purse or scrip, trusting in the Lord. Did he ever forsake me? Never, no never. I always was provided for, for which I feel to praise God my Heavenly Father.

(John Taylor, *The Gospel Kingdom: Selections from the Writings and Discourses of John Taylor*, ed. G. Homer Durham [1943], 234)

Blessings of Missionary Work

Said President Kimball, "Missionary work, like the tithing, will pour out blessings, as Malachi said, so many blessings that there'll hardly be room enough to receive them" . . . I believe that. Almost every conceivable spiritual blessing is in some way related to full-time missionary service. . . .

I was set apart for a calling by President Alma Sonne of the European Mission. At the conclusion of the blessing, I thanked Elder Sonne for the beautiful and inspiring words he had spoken. He graciously accepted my expression of gratitude; however, he placed his hand upon my shoulder, looked intently into my eyes, and said, "Elder Asay, I had the power and right to say what I said, but remember, you will write your own blessing by the way you live and serve." Then he added, "Go and write the best blessing that has ever been written." (Carlos E. Asay, *The Seven M's of Missionary Service: Proclaiming the Gospel as a Member or Full-time Missionary* [1996])

Missionary Work Requires Sacrifice

I pray that the Spirit of God may burn in the bosoms of the Latter-day Saints; that the love and charity our Father has for his children may be ours; that we may rejoice when we see his children understanding the truth and that we may be willing to make what may sometimes be termed a sacrifice; that we may be willing to make the investment to bless our kind, going forth with all our might to bring light and salvation to the children of men by preaching unto them the restored gospel of our Lord. (George Albert Smith, *The Teachings of George Albert Smith* [1996], 159)

The Power of Commitment

A truly committed person does not falter in the face of adversity. Until one is committed, there is a chance to hesitate, to go off in another direction, or to be ineffective. Members within our ranks who are committed to living the gospel of Jesus Christ will not be affected by the rationale of hecklers. . . .

Those who are firmly committed to living the gospel of Jesus Christ will not be confused, confounded, or led astray.

If we profess to be Latter-day Saints, let us be committed to living like Latter-day Saints, using Jesus Christ as our master teacher.

It is not too late to commit ourselves to living the gospel totally while here on earth. Each day we must be committed to lofty Christian performance because commitment to the truths of the gospel of Jesus Christ is essential to our eternal joy and happiness. The time to commit and recommit is now. (Marvin J. Ashton, *Be of Good Cheer* [1987], 51, 53)

Learning by Faith

How does one get "learning by faith"? One prophet explains the process: First, one must arouse his faculties and experiment on the words of the Lord and desire to believe. Let this desire work in you until you believe in a manner that you can give place even to a portion of the word of the Lord. Then, like a planted seed, it must be cultivated and not resist the Spirit of the Lord, which is that which lighteneth everyone born into the world. You can then begin to feel within yourselves that it must be good, for it enlarges your soul and enlightens your understanding and, like the fruit of the tree in

Lehi's vision, it becomes delicious to the taste. (See Alma 32) (Harold B. Lee, *Stand Ye in Holy Places* [1974], 358)

Becoming a Latter-Day Saint

A person is a true Latter-day Saint if he (or she) is so inwardly, if his conversion is that of the heart, in the spirit, whose praise is not from men for outward acts but from God for the inward desires of his heart.

As we seek to determine whether we have become true Latter-day Saints—inwardly as well as outwardly—it soon becomes apparent that the critical element is progress, not longevity. The question is not how much time we have logged, but how far we have progressed toward perfection. As Elder Neal A. Maxwell has said, "Life is not lineal, but experiential, not chronological, but developmental" (*Ensign*, December 1986, 23). The issue is not what we have done but what we have become. And what we have become is the result of more than our actions. It is also the result of our attitudes, our motives, and our desires. Each of these is an ingredient of the pure heart. (Dallin H. Oaks, *Pure in Heart* [1988], 138)

Teaching with Power and Authority

Jesus, who taught "as one having authority" (Matthew 7:29), was and ever will be the greatest teacher. He provides the perfect model for us to follow as we strive to improve our own teaching skills. We are to teach by the Spirit (see D&C 42:14 and 50:17–22), "according to the office wherewith I have appointed you," the Lord says (D&C 38:23). As we strive to do so, we will receive wondrous blessings of power and comprehension, far beyond our mortal capacities. "Teach ye diligently and my grace shall attend you, that you may be instructed more perfectly in theory, in principle, in doctrine, in the law of the gospel, in all things that pertain unto the kingdom of God, . . . that ye may be prepared in all things . . . to magnify the calling whereunto I have called you, and the mission with which I have commissioned you." (D&C 88:78, 80) (Alexander B. Morrison, *Feed My Sheep: Leadership Ideas for Latter-day Shepherds* [1992], 67)

After All We Can Do

What is meant by "after all we can do"? "After all we can do" includes extending our best effort. "After all we can do" includes living His commandments.

"After all we can do" includes loving our fellowmen and praying for those who regard us as their adversary. "After all we can do" means clothing the naked, feeding the hungry, visiting the sick and giving "succor [to] those who stand in need of [our] succor" (Mosiah 4:15)—remembering that what we do unto one of the least of God's children, we do unto Him (see Matthew 25:34–40; D&C 42:38). "After all we can do" means leading chaste, clean, pure lives, being scrupulously honest in all our dealings and treating others the way we would want to be treated. (Ezra Taft Benson, *The Teachings of Ezra Taft Benson* [1988], 354)

Missionary Service Brings Peace and Happiness beyond Understanding

It is not an easy task; it is not a pleasant thing, perhaps, to be called out into the world, to leave our dear ones, but I say to you that it will purchase for those who are faithful, for those who discharge that obligation as they may be required, peace and happiness beyond all understanding, and will prepare them that, in due time, when life's labor is complete, they will stand in the presence of their Maker, accepted of him because of what they have done. (George Albert Smith, *The Teachings of George Albert Smith* [1996], 159)

The Power of Faith in Jesus Christ

"Thy faith hath made thee whole" or words like unto it occur throughout the scriptures (Mark 5:34). One of the gifts of the Spirit is faith to be healed (see D&C 46:19). And thus we gain insight, as mentioned before, why the early Apostles entreated the Lord to increase their faith (see Luke 17:5). President Hinckley has said, "If there is any one thing you and I need in this world it is faith, that dynamic, powerful, marvelous element by which, as Paul declared, the very worlds were framed (Hebrews 11:3). . . . Faith—the kind of faith that moves one to get on his knees and plead with the Lord and then get on his feet and go to work—is an asset beyond compare, even in the acquisition of secular knowledge." (*Teachings of Gordon B. Hinckley* [1997], 186)

The Blessings of the Comforter

Because the Holy Spirit speaks peace to the hearts of weary and disconsolate mortals, he is called the Comforter. He brings peace and solace, love and quiet enjoyment, the joy of redemption and the hope of eternal life. These words of promise are given to all who receive the gift of the Holy Ghost: "Therefore it is given to abide in you; the record of heaven; the Comforter; the peaceable things of immortal glory; the truth of all things; that which quickeneth all things, which maketh alive all things; that which knoweth all things, and hath all power, according to wisdom, mercy, truth, justice, and judgment" (Moses 6:61). How glorious is the word we have received! How wondrous is the Spirit that dwells in faithful hearts! (Bruce R. McConkie, *A New Witness for the Articles of Faith* [1985], 268)

Poor in Spirit

To be poor in spirit is to feel yourselves as the spiritually needy, ever dependent upon the Lord for your clothes, your food, and the air you breathe, your health, your life; realizing that no day should pass without fervent prayer of thanksgiving, for guidance and forgiveness and strength sufficient for each day's need. If a youth realizes his spiritual need, when in dangerous places where his very life is at stake, he may be drawn close to the fountain of truth and be prompted by the Spirit of the Lord in his hour of greatest trial. . . . Thus, if in your humility you sense your spiritual need, you are made ready for adoption into the "Church of the First Born, and to become the elect of God." (Harold B. Lee, *Decisions for Successful Living* [1973], 57–58)

Spiritual Gifts

Spiritual gifts properly sought, properly received, and properly shared will establish faith, profit those who love God, and edify the Church. Elder Bruce R. McConkie provides this statement of purpose: "Their purpose is to enlighten, encourage, and edify the faithful so that they will inherit peace in this life and be guided toward eternal life in the world to come. Their presence is proof of the divinity of the Lord's work; where they are not found, there the Church and kingdom of God is not." (Carlos E. Asay, *In the Lord's Service: A Guide to Spiritual Development* [1990], 125)

Spiritual Discernment

There is no perfect operation of the power of discernment without revelation. Thereby even "the thoughts and intents of the heart" are made known (D& C 33:1; Heb. 4:12). Where the Saints are concerned—since they have received the right to the constant companionship of the Holy Ghost—the Lord expects them to discern, not only between the righteous and the wicked, but between false and true philosophies, educational theories, sciences, political concepts, and social schemes. Unfortunately, in many instances, even good men hearken to "the tradition of their fathers" (D& C 93:39) and rely on the learning of the world rather than the revelations of the Lord, so that they do not enjoy the full play of the spirit of discernment. (Bruce R. McConkie, *Mormon Doctrine*, 2nd ed. [1966], 197)

Blessings of the Holy Ghost

The Holy Ghost can even help us to know what to pray for. "He that asketh in the Spirit asketh according to the will of God; wherefore it is done even as he asketh" (D&C 46:30). If we can receive the Spirit through a prayer of faith, we can then ask "in the Spirit," which will help us to ask "according to the will of God." Such prayers are always answered.

The Spirit can aid the process of communication in other ways:

> *Likewise the Spirit also helpeth our infirmities: for we know not what we should pray for as we ought: but the Spirit itself maketh intercession for us with groanings which cannot be uttered.*
>
> *And he that searcheth the hearts knoweth what is the mind of the Spirit, because he maketh intercession for the saints according to the will of God." (Romans 8:26–27)*

It's evident that the Spirit will help us by revealing that for which we should pray. (Gene R. Cook, *Receiving Answers to Our Prayers* [1996], 70)

The Blessings of the Spirit Can Come If You Are Clean and Pure

If you would have the blessings of the Spirit of the Lord to be with you, you must keep your body—

the temple of God, as the Apostle Paul speaks of it—clean and pure. In other words, your spiritual housekeeping must always be properly done if you would invite the Spirit of the Lord, for the gift of the Holy Ghost with which you were blessed at the time of your baptism will not be yours unless you keep your body fit to receive this blessing. (Harold B. Lee, *Ye Are the Light of the World: Selected Sermons and Writings of Harold B. Lee* [1974])

The Spirit of Truth

In such settings, experience also suggests the importance not only of meekness but also of the presence of the Spirit. Neither advice-giver nor circumstances can be perfect. Only the Spirit can leap across such deficiencies and convey the message lovingly and yet forcefully. The Lord told the elders of the Church in 1831, "Why is it that ye cannot understand and know, that he that receiveth the word by the Spirit of truth receiveth it as it is preached by the Spirit of truth? Wherefore, he that preacheth and he that receiveth, understand one another, and both are edified and rejoice together" (D&C 50:21–22).

Absent mutual meekness, the counsel given may not only go unheeded, but, in fact, may even be resented. (Neal A. Maxwell, *Meek and Lowly* [1987], 57)

Set Your Goals

As we search for good causes, we must consider our own needs, but also we must live in compliance with gospel teachings.

President Spencer W. Kimball at the Regional Representatives Seminar of April 3, 1975, said, "I believe in goals, but I believe that the individual should set his own. Goals should always be made to a point that will make us reach and strain. Success should not necessarily be gauged by always reaching the goal set, but by progress and attainment."

In setting our own goals we need to examine our own needs and abilities. The direction in which we are moving is more important than where we are at the moment. Goal-setting should cause us to stretch as we make our way. (Marvin J. Ashton, *Be of Good Cheer* [1987], 49)

What Is Your Quest?

If you seek pleasure for its own sake, when you find it, it may be a head of wheat that has been smitten by "smut"; *but seek to share joy with others, or to make somebody else happy, and you will find your own soul radiant with the joy you wished for another.*

This guiding, ever-present thought was expressed by Jesus when he said:

Seek ye first the kingdom of God, and his righteousness; and all these things shall be added unto you (Matthew 6:33).

What a man is may largely be determined by his dominant quest. (David O. McKay, *Man May Know for Himself: Teachings of President David O. McKay*, comp. Clare Middlemiss [1967], 179)

The Joy of Repentance

Remember, it is complete deliverance from the tortures of a guilt-ridden soul that we seek. The Prophet Alma says he wandered "through much tribulation, repenting nigh unto death," feeling he was being consumed by an everlasting burning (Mosiah 27:28). Repentance is not easy. "Godly sorrow" brings one to the depth of humility. This is why the gift of forgiveness is so sweet and draws the transgressor so close to the Savior with a special bond of affection. (J. Richard Clarke, in *Repentance* [1990], 92)

A Spirit of Thanksgiving

Elder James E. Talmage once observed that "God requires thanksgiving, praise and worship, not for His gratification as the recipient of adulation, but for the good of His children" (*Sunday Night Talks by Radio,* 2d ed., Salt Lake City: The Church of Jesus Christ of Latter-Day Saints, 1931, 486). The good we receive by developing a thankful heart is immeasurable. It cultivates feelings of reverence for God and thereby opens our souls to the influence of the Holy Spirit. It allows us to find joy in the here and now. A thankful heart allows us to face trials firm in the knowledge of our Heavenly Father's love for us. I like the words of Carolyn Wright concerning the power of gratitude: "The grateful heart," she says, "sits at a continual feast." ("The Thankful Heart," *Ensign*, March 1994, 26–27)

Compare Your Time as a Missionary to the Past—Offer a Prayer of Gratitude

I was called on a mission to the Southern States in the days when great bitterness motivated some of the people who lived there. The most of them were good men and women, but there were a few who objected to the gospel of Jesus Christ being taught as the Lord desires us to teach it. Some of our missionaries were brutally whipped. During the period of time before I went there, several were killed. I had the experience myself of lying in bed while the bullets whistled overhead. A mob surrounded the building where we were sleeping and fired into the four corners. Splinters fell over us, but nobody was hurt. I labored under the direction of Elder J. Golden Kimball. He was a great mission president. I came home and continued my life work, having been benefited by the experience of my missionary career. (George Albert Smith, *The Teachings of George Albert Smith* [1996], 160)

We Should Be Patient and Forgiving of Ourselves As Well As Others

It has always struck me as being sad that those among us who would not think of reprimanding our neighbor, much less a total stranger, for mistakes that have been made or weaknesses that might be evident, will nevertheless be cruel and unforgiving to themselves. When the scriptures say to judge righteously, that means with fairness and compassion and charity. That's how we must judge ourselves. We need to be patient and forgiving of ourselves, just as we must be patient and forgiving of others. . . .

It may not surprise you to know that God loves us more than we love ourselves. We are his creation, spirit children of a celestial birth, and we stand in the image of him whom we rightly call our Father. We ought never to be destructive in our criticism of others, but perhaps our greatest caution needs to be regarding the tendency to be destructive in the criticism we apply to ourselves. (Howard W. Hunter, *The Teachings of Howard W. Hunter,* ed. Clyde J. Williams [1997], 34–35)

You Are the Messengers

And who shall carry the message to the world? Those to whom it is first revealed and those who first believe its doctrines and obey its ordinances. . . . That ensign, the fulness of the everlasting gospel, has now been raised; and that trumpet, the gospel trumpet, is now sounding its clarion call. This is the day when the root of Jesse is standing "for an ensign of the people"; when "the Lord shall set his hand again the second time to recover the remnant of his people," from all the lands and islands of their dispersion. (Bruce R. McConkie, *A New Witness for the Articles of Faith* [1985], 536)

Be Not Weary in Well Doing

All have the duty to share the gospel with others and to serve formally and informally as missionaries. All have a duty to identify their deceased ancestors and to help bring to them the blessings of the temple. All should diligently strive to be temporally prepared and to care for the poor and the needy. All should seek to strengthen those who are less active in the Church and to magnify their callings in their wards and stakes by giving faithful and devoted service.

These are some of our duties. They may not always be exciting or even enjoyable, but they are important. They will refine the spirit and strengthen the soul. They will aid the work of the Lord in great measure.

The Lord has told us, "Be not weary in well-doing" (D&C 64:33). Being true to one's duty is the mark of a true disciple of the Lord and a child of God. (Joseph B. Wirthlin, *Finding Peace in Our Lives* [1995], 94)

We Are Justified and Made Just When We Accept the Lord's Infinite Atonement

Much more then, being now justified by his blood, we shall be saved from wrath through him. (Romans 5:9)

We may become "just" or justified (as when a printer lines up the edges of crooked margins; when all the lines are straight, the printing is "justified") when we demonstrate sufficient repentance to receive the Savior's mercy. The demands of justice are then satisfied. This may be the "*justification* through the grace of our Lord and Savior Jesus Christ," which "is just and true." (D&C 20:30) (Bruce C. Hafen, *The Broken Heart: Applying the Atonement to Life's Experiences* [1989], 166)

The Lord Requires the Heart and a Willing Mind

The Lord declared that he requires "the heart and a willing mind; and the willing and obedient shall eat the good of the land of Zion in these last days" (D&C 64:34).

A wise man of experience observed: Men will work hard for money. They will work harder for other men. But men will work hardest of all when they are dedicated to a cause. Until willingness overflows obligation, men fight as conscripts rather than following the flag as patriots. Duty is never worthily performed until it is performed by one who would gladly do more if only he could.

Man does not by himself run the race of life. When we help another in his race of life, we really serve our God. King Benjamin stated the principle so beautifully, "When ye are in the service of your fellow beings ye are only in the service of your God." (Mosiah 2:17) (Thomas S. Monson, *Pathways to Perfection* [1973], 278)

The Lord Jesus Christ Lives

I know, as well as I know that I live and look into your faces, that Jesus Christ lives, and he is the Redeemer of the world, that he arose from the dead with a tangible body, and still has that real body which Thomas touched when he thrust his hands into his side and felt the wound of the spear, and also the prints of the nails in his hands. [John 20:26–29.] I know by the witness and the revelations of God to me that Thomas told the truth. I know that Joseph Smith told the truth, for mine eyes have seen. For in the visions of the Lord to my soul, I have seen Christ's face, I have heard his voice. I know that he lives, that he is the Redeemer of the World, and that as he arose from the dead, a tangible and real individual, so shall all men arise in the resurrection from the dead. [D&C 88:29–32.] (Melvin J. Ballard, in Conference Report, Apr. 1920, 40–41)

Give Your All

By putting everything we have on the altar of the Lord and not waiting for Him to give us a receipt, we show our submissiveness. Otherwise our giving may become linked with expecting recognition or with soliciting proof of the Lord's appreciation. After all, one day He will give everything to the faithful (D&C 84:38). God, who is perfect in His gratitude, "delights to honor those who serve" Him (D&C 76:5). Mortal recognition is so fleeting, but God remembers always those who remember Him. (Neal A. Maxwell, *Not My Will, But Thine* [1998], 96)

Line upon Line, Precept upon Precept

This attitude and practice of obedience completes the circle in the pattern of hearing the Lord's voice. Our obedience to his instructions—both general and personalized—qualifies us to receive additional instructions, and thus we continue from truth to truth, learning and doing all that the Lord requires. By this means we grow "line upon line, precept upon precept" (D&C 98:12; also see Isaiah 28:10, 13) "unto a perfect man, unto the measure of the stature of the fulness of Christ" (Ephesians 4:13). (Gene R. Cook, *Searching the Scriptures: Bringing Power to Your Personal and Family Study* [1997], 109)

Every Day Can Be the Best Day

It is our privilege to say, every day in our lives, "That is the best day I ever lived." Never let a day so pass that you will have cause to say, "I will live better to-morrow," and I will promise you, in the name of the Lord Jesus, that your lives will be as a well of water springing up to everlasting life. You will have his Spirit to dwell in you continually, and your eyes will be open to see, your ears to hear, and your understandings to comprehend.

He gives a little to his humble followers today, and if they improve upon it, tomorrow he will give them a little more, and the next day a little more. (Brigham Young, *Discourses of Brigham Young,* sel. John A. Widtsoe [1954], 90)

Do As Jesus Would Do

In his novel, a Christian minister presents his congregation with this interesting challenge: "I want [a] volunteer . . . who will pledge themselves, earnestly and honestly for an entire year, not to do anything without first asking the question, 'What would Jesus do?'. . . Our aim will be to act just as He would if He [were] in our places, regardless of immediate results. In other words, we propose to follow Jesus' steps as closely and as literally as we believe He taught His disciples to do" (Charles M. Sheldon, *In His Steps*, New York: Grosset & Dunlap, 1935, pp. 15–16). . . .

Do we catch the significance of this thought? We demonstrate the depth of our love for the Savior when we care enough to seek out the suffering among us and attend to their needs. (J. Richards Clarke, *Love* [1986], 55–56)

The Lord Is Empowered by Law

"Mormonism" has taught me that God holds Himself accountable to law even as He expects us to do. He has set us the example in obedience to law. I know that to say this would have been heresy a few decades ago. But we have the divine word for it [see D&C 82:10]. He operates by law and not by arbitrariness or caprice. He is no tyrant to be propitiated and placated by honeyed words. He cannot be moved by wordy oratory. He is not a judge sitting to be influenced by the specious pleas of crafty advocates; and yet there is an eloquence that moves Him; there is a plea that influences Him. The eloquence of prayer from a broken heart and a contrite spirit prevails with him. . . .

He will take all circumstances into account and will give unto every man that which is his. (James E. Talmage, in Conference Report, Apr. 1930, 96)

Ultimate Blessings to the Believer

The Gospel of Christ is the power of God unto salvation unto all those who believe it; but it is not the power of salvation to any man who does not believe it. . . .

Notwithstanding He was crucified for the sins of the world and His blood was shed for the redemption of mankind; notwithstanding all this, no man on the earth will ever be saved by the Gospel unless he believes it. A man will never be saved in unbelief. The Gospel is not the power of God unto salvation to the unbeliever, but it is destined to save all who believe and obey it. (Hyrum M. Smith, in Conference Report, Apr. 1904, 97)

The Lord Will Help You

And whoso receiveth you, there I will be also, for I will go before your face. I will be on your right hand and on your left, and my Spirit shall be in your hearts, and mine angels round about you, to bear you up. (D&C 84:88)

There is not anything desirable that you will not be able to do with the aid and the help of the Lord, and every gift and power will be with you to accomplish his work if you will do your full part. (Ezra Taft Benson, *A Labor of Love: The 1946 European Mission of Ezra Taft Benson* [1989], 238)

We Are Part of the Lord's Kingdom

God bless you, my beloved associates in this great work. We are all in this together. None of us can slip down without taking the whole Church down somewhat. None of us can do better without lifting the whole Church somewhat. You are important. Everyone is important. We are all a part of it. We can do a little better. I pray that we will work at it just a little harder, with a little more devotion, a little more love, a little more prayer, a little more enthusiasm. This is the Savior's work. This is not my church, it is the Savior's church. He stands at the head. We are merely here to do His bidding, to listen to His voice, and try to give expression to it the best way we know how. (Gordon B. Hinckley, *Teachings of Gordon B. Hinckley* [1997], 137)

Blessings of Accepting the Gospel

As a universal gift flowing from the atonement of Christ, the Resurrection will clothe with a permanent, perfected, restored body every spirit ever born into mortality. Furthermore, for every person who accepts the principles and ordinances of the gospel, that person's body will be something of a robe of righteousness. Therein is the redemption of the soul, and therein is a fulness of joy throughout all eternity, including, in its highest order, "a fulness and a continuation of the seeds forever and ever." (Jeffrey R. Holland, *Christ and the New Covenant: The Messianic Message of the Book of Mormon* [1997], 244)

Faithfulness in Keeping the Commandments

To be faithful is to strive each day to keep the commandments, to hunger and thirst after righteousness, to plead for divine guidance, and to seek for and listen to the still, small voice. To be faithful is to listen to and act upon the admonitions of the prophets, to humbly, obediently, and gladly follow their instructions, remembering that the voice of His servants is the same as the Lord's (see D&C 1:38). Faithfulness in keeping the commandments thus is not passive; it is active, joyful, anxious engagement in good causes, reverence for righteousness, an eye single to the glory of God. It embodies both commitment and action, and it must be seen within the context of enduring to the end while steadfastly pushing forward, feasting on the words of Christ. (See 2 Nephi 31:20) (Alexander B. Morrison, *Feed My Sheep: Leadership Ideas for Latter-day Shepherds* [1992], 63)

Prayer and Fasting

I am confident that as leaders we do not do enough fasting and praying. If you want to get the spirit of your office and calling as a new president of a quorum, a new high councilman, a new bishop—try fasting for a period. I don't mean just missing one meal, then eating twice as much the next meal. I mean really fasting, and praying during that period. It will do more to give you the real spirit of your office and calling and permit the Spirit to operate through you than anything I know. (Ezra Taft Benson, *The Teachings of Ezra Taft Benson* [1988], 331–32)

Love One Another

True love is a process. True love requires personal action. Love must be continuing to be real. Love takes time. . . .

We must at regular and appropriate intervals speak and reassure others of our love and the long time it takes to prove it by our actions. Real love does take time. The Great Shepherd had the same thoughts in mind when he taught, "If ye love me, *keep* my commandments" (John 14:15; italics added) and "If ye love me *feed* my sheep" (John 21:16; italics added). Love demands action if it is to be continuing. Love is a process. Love is not a declaration. Love is not an announcement. Love is not a passing fancy. Love is not an expediency. Love is not a convenience. "If ye love me, keep my commandments" and "If ye love me feed my sheep" are God-given proclamations that should remind us we can often best show our love through the processes of *feeding* and *keeping.* (Marvin J. Ashton, "Love Takes Time," *Ensign*, Nov. 1975, 108)

Repentance Is the Only Way

Now, my brethren, you who have sinned, repent of your sins. I can say to you in regard to Jesus and the atonement (it is so written, and I firmly believe it), that Christ has died for all. He has paid the full debt, whether you receive the gift or not. But if we continue to sin, to lie, steal, bear false witness, we must repent of and forsake that sin to have the full efficacy of the blood of Christ. Without this it will be of no effect; repentance must come, in order that the atonement may prove a benefit to us. Let all who are doing wrong cease doing wrong; live no longer in transgression, no matter of what kind; but live every day of your lives according to the revelations given. (Brigham Young, *Discourses of Brigham Young,* sel. John A. Widtsoe [1954], 156)

Live Up to Your Privileges

My dear brethren, may we diligently seek to learn the doctrine of the holy priesthood, may we strengthen our testimonies line upon line by receiving the revelations of the Spirit, and may we find true joy in daily priesthood service. As we do these things, we will begin to live up to our potential and privileges as priesthood holders, and we will be able to "do all things through Christ which strengtheneth [us]" (Philippans 4:13). Of this I bear testimony as an Apostle of the Lord and leave you my blessing in the sacred name of Jesus Christ, amen. (Dieter F. Uchtdorf, "Your Potential, Your Privilege," *Ensign*, May 2011)

The Lord Blesses Us to the Degree That We Keep the Commandments

The Lord will bless us to the degree to which we keep His commandments. Nephi put this principle in a tremendous orbit when he said, "For we labor diligently to write, to persuade our children, and also our brethren, to believe in Christ, and to be reconciled to God; for we know that it is by grace that we are saved, after all we can do" (2 Nephi 25:23). The Savior's blood, His atonement, will save us, but only after we have done all we can to save ourselves by keeping His commandments. (Harold B. Lee, *The Teachings of Harold B. Lee*, ed. Clyde J. Williams [1996], 186)

Pray Always

We have this instruction from our risen Lord as He ministered among the Nephite people on this Western Hemisphere: "Ye must watch and pray always, lest ye be tempted by the devil, and ye are led away captive by him. . . . Ye must watch and pray always lest ye enter into temptation; for Satan desireth to have you, that he may sift you as wheat. Therefore ye must always pray unto the

Father in my name; and whatsoever ye shall ask the Father in my name, which is right, believing that ye shall receive, behold it shall be given unto you." (Book of Mormon, 3 Nephi 18:15, 18–21)

Here are five ways to improve our communication with our Heavenly Father.

1. *We should pray frequently.* . . .

2. *We should find an appropriate place where we can meditate and pray.* . . .

3. *We should prepare ourselves for prayer.* . . .

4. *Our prayers should be meaningful and pertinent.* . . .

5. *After making a request through prayer, we have a responsibility to assist in its being granted.* (Ezra Taft Benson, *Come unto Christ* [1983], 25)

The Temple Should Be Our Ultimate Earthly Goal

Let us truly be a temple-attending and a temple-loving people. We should hasten to the temple as frequently, yet prudently, as our personal circumstances allow. We should go not only for our kindred dead but also for the personal blessing of temple worship, for the sanctity and safety that are within those hallowed and consecrated walls. As we attend the temple, we learn more richly and deeply the purpose of life and the significance of the atoning sacrifice of the Lord Jesus Christ. Let us make the temple, with temple worship and temple covenants and temple marriage, our ultimate earthly goal and the supreme mortal experience. (Howard W. Hunter, *The Teachings of Howard W. Hunter*, ed. Clyde J. Williams [1997], 236)

Freedom through Righteousness

We often speak of our freedoms. There is no freedom like the freedom of righteousness. The penalty of sin is slavery and death. He who is the victim of his own evil conduct is in reality much more a slave than the cowering subjects of the most dictatorial despot.

If America would remain mighty, she must have the strength of sobriety, of chastity and virtue, of honesty and integrity, and power of true spirituality. If she would be strong, America must enjoy—in addition to her political freedoms—those other freedoms which are as essential to her welfare as any of the liberties listed in the Bill of Rights. (Mark E. Peterson, in Conference Report, Oct. 1947, 107–8)

Sacrifice Is at the Very Center of the Gospel

Sacrifice is the very essence of religion; it is the keystone of happy home life, the basis of true friendship, the foundation of peaceful community living, of sound relations among people and nations. . . .

Without sacrifice there is no true worship of God. I become increasingly convinced of that every day. "The Father gave his Son, and the Son gave his life," and we do not worship unless we give—give of our substance, give of our time, give of our strength, give of our talent, give of our faith, give of our testimonies. . . .

A religion which requires devotion, which asks for sacrifice, which demands discipline, also enjoys the loyalty of its membership and the interest and respect of others. (Gordon B. Hinckley, *Teachings of Gordon B. Hinckley* [1997], 565)

Faithfulness and Diligence

I want to bear record . . . that there is no other way of retaining the spirit of this work and the fellowship of the Holy Ghost than through faithfulness and diligence in observing to keep the commandments of the Lord. The individual who will be humble all the day long and strive to keep the commandments of the Lord will never apostatize or become dissatisfied, but he or she will be preserved in the truth, and by and by will sit down in the mansions of the Father, to enjoy the blessings of eternal life. People who are spiritually-minded are devoted to the work. They pay their tithes and their offerings; they go to the ward meetings and to the stake meetings, and they are willing to devote their time, their talents and their all for the building up of the kingdom of God on the earth. (Marriner W. Merrill, in Conference Report, Apr. 1902, 40)

Trial of Your Faith

Thus there ought to be expectations that in this laboratory of life we will actually see each other in the process of being remodeled, sometimes succeeding and sometimes failing. We will obviously be aware of others who are also in the "furnace of affliction." However, we will not always have a smooth, ready answer to the question, "Why me?" "Why now?" "Why this?"—for as Moroni observed, "Ye receive no witness until *after* the trial of your faith." (Ether 12:6; italics added)

As we see ourselves, and others, passing through fiery trials, the wisdom of Peter, who had his own share of fiery trials, is very useful: "Beloved, think it not strange concerning the fiery trial which is to try you, as though some strange thing happened unto you." (1 Peter 4:12) (Neal A. Maxwell, *All These Things Shall Give Thee Experience* [1979], 44)

Serve with Purity of Heart

If our service is to be most efficacious, it must be accomplished for the love of God and the love of his children. . . .

This principle—that our service should be for the love of God and the love of fellowmen rather than for personal advantage or any other lesser motive—is admittedly a high standard. The Savior must have seen it so, since he joined his commandment for selfless and complete love directly with the ideal of perfection . . . "Be ye therefore perfect, even as your Father which is in heaven is perfect." (Matthew 5:48). . . .

Service with all of our heart and mind is a high challenge for all of us. Such service must be free of selfish ambition. It must be motivated only by the pure love of Christ. . . .

I know that God expects us to work to purify our hearts and our thoughts so that we may serve one another for the highest and best reason, the pure love of Christ. (Dallin H. Oaks, "Why Do We Serve?" *Ensign*, Oct. 1984, 16)

Learning by Faith and Revelation

Latter-day Saints affirm the reality and effectiveness of learning by faith and revelation.

The Lord's way of revealing himself and of communicating understanding about the doctrines and ordinances of his gospel is revelation by the Holy Ghost, the Spirit of God. Indeed, the prophet Jacob declared the impossibility of uninspired man's understanding God: "No man knoweth of his ways save it be revealed unto him; wherefore, brethren, despise not the revelations of God" (Jacob 4:8). Similarly, the apostle Paul taught, "The things of God knoweth no man, except he has the Spirit of God." (JST 1 Corinthians 2:11) (Dallin H. Oaks, *The Lord's Way* [1991], 19)

The Priesthood and Your Righteousness

His Holy Priesthood he has caused to be bestowed upon many good men, and he has defined the nature of that priesthood and told us that the rights of the priesthood can be "handled only upon the principles of righteousness" and that "no power or influence can . . . be maintained by virtue of the priesthood only by persuasion, by long-suffering, by gentleness and meekness, and by love unfeigned." He has admonished all men who bear his priesthood to cultivate "charity towards all men, and to the household of faith, and let virtue garnish thy thoughts unceasingly; then shall thy confidence wax strong in the presence of God; and the doctrine of the priesthood shall distil upon thy soul as the dews from heaven." What a precious gift this bestowal of divine power is, and our Lord has generously made provision that every man who is worthy may receive and use it for the blessing of his fellow men. (Stephen L Richards, *Where Is Wisdom?* [1955], 321)

Then They Shall Be Gods

The great and grand secret of salvation, which we should continually seek to understand through our faithfulness, is the continuation of the lives. Those of the Latter-day Saints who will continue to follow after the revelations and commandments of God to do them, who are found to be obedient in all things, continually advancing little by little towards perfection and the knowledge of God, they, when they enter the spirit world and receive their bodies, will be able to advance faster in the things pertaining to the knowledge of the Gods, and will continue onward and upward until they become Gods, even the sons of God. This I say is the great secret of the hereafter, to continue in the lives forever, and forever, which is the greatest of all gifts God has ever bestowed upon his children. We all have it within our reach, we can all attain to that perfected and exalted state if we will embrace its principles and practice them in our every-day life. (Brigham Young, in *Journal of Discourses*, 18:260)

Divine Duty

It is our duty, divinely imposed, to continue urgently and militantly to carry forward our missionary work. We must continue to call missionaries and send them out to preach the gospel, which was never more needed than now, which is the only remedy for the tragic ills that now afflict the world, and which alone can bring peace and brotherly love back amongst the peoples of the earth.

This is not a matter of our own choosing. It is not something that has been devised by man. The

Lord has made it clear to us, my brethren, that the responsibility is ours, as holders of the priesthood, to carry this message of the restored gospel to the people of the world. (Ezra Taft Benson, *The Teachings of Ezra Taft Benson* [1988], 180–81)

Our Missionaries Go Out to Teach the Gospel of Jesus Christ

Today as I realize the need of faith, when I think of the multitude of our Father's sons and daughters who are in darkness, I realize that each of us ought to be putting forth every possible effort to carry this message forward if possible here at home and abroad. To that end we have been given divine authority, so that when an elder of this church goes into the world he does not go to be instructed of those who have been educated in the seminaries of learning necessarily, but he goes with the information he may possess. He may have a trained mind, he may possess the learning that he has obtained in our great universities, but the thing that he possesses that is important to the world when he goes out to teach is a knowledge that God lives, a testimony of the divine mission of Jesus Christ; and to that end we have been called and chosen and set apart. (George

Albert Smith, *The Teachings of George Albert Smith* [1996], 162)

Contention Is of the Devil

In a recent conference message, Elder Russell M. Nelson expressed concern "that contention is becoming accepted as a way of life." In the press, on television, and in various aspects of political and public affairs, the *modus operandi* is contention. We live in an environment of contention. But, as Elder Nelson reminds us, contention is not the Lord's way: "How easy it is, yet how wrong it is, to allow habits of contention to pervade matters of spiritual significance, because contention is forbidden by divine decree: 'The Lord God hath commanded that men should not . . . envy; that they should not have malice; that they should not contend one with another.'" (2 Nephi 26:32)

The Savior is the "Prince of Peace," and the devil is the "father of contention" (3 Nephi 11:29). In the language of Elder Bruce R. McConkie, "The Spirit of the Lord leads to harmony and unity and agreement and oneness. The spirit of the devil champions division and debate and contention and disunity." (Dallin H. Oaks, *The Lord's Way* [1991], 150)

The Enabling Infinite Atonement

And reflecting upon the great atoning sacrifice that was made by the Son of God, for the redemption of the world;

And the great and wonderful love made manifest by the Father and the Son in the coming of the Redeemer into the world. (D&C 138:2–3)

Finally, while pursuing our individual submissiveness, we are helped immensely when we ponder the infinite Atonement. God did not spare His Beloved Son from the anguish of these perfecting experiences. Jesus Christ has been, is, and will be our empathic Advocate with the Father. Not only is He our Advocate, but He helps us through our individual ordeals. By His own suffering He was perfected, including in His capacity to help us with our individual suffering. (Alma 7:11–12) (Neal A. Maxwell, *Not My Will, But Thine* [1998], 3)

Fishers of Men

Now, your responsibility to touch lives might seem overwhelming. You can take heart that you were called by the Savior. . . .

He will make you a fisher of men, however inadequate you may feel now. It won't be done by a mysterious process. It will be the natural result of your choosing to follow him. Just think about what you must do to be a fisher of men, to touch lives with faith for him. You will need to love the people you serve. You will need to be humble and full of hope. You will need to have the Holy Ghost as your companion to know when to speak and what to say and how to testify. (Henry B. Eyring, *To Draw Closer to God: A Collection of Discourses* [1997], 190)

The Blessings of Meekness

Heavenly power can be accessed only by those who are Christlike; it is a power whose continued availability is maintained by meekness along with the other virtues. Nor can we have the loving empathy or understanding mercy necessary for true discipleship without meekness. (Neal A. Maxwell, *Meek and Lowly* [Salt Lake City: Deseret Book, 1987], 85)

Discipleship is not simply surviving and enduring; discipleship is a pressing forward, a creative Christianity. Discipleship does not wait to be acted upon, but instead acts upon men and circumstances to make things better. . . . True discipleship is for volunteers only. Only volunteers will trust the Guide sufficiently to follow Him in the dangerous ascent which only He can lead. (*The Neal A. Maxwell Quote Book*, ed. Cory H. Maxwell [Salt Lake City: Bookcraft, 1997], 91)

The Nobleness of Forgiveness

If we have been wronged or injured, forgiveness means to blot it completely from our minds. To forgive and forget is an ageless counsel. "To be wronged or robbed," said the Chinese philosopher Confucius, "is nothing unless you continue to remember it."

The injuries inflicted by neighbors, by relatives, or by spouses are generally of a minor nature, at least at first. We must forgive them. Since the Lord is so merciful, must not we be? "Blessed are the merciful, for they shall obtain mercy" (3 Nephi 12:7) is another version of the golden rule. "All manner of sin and blasphemy shall be forgiven unto men" said the Lord, "but the blasphemy against the Holy Ghost shall not be forgiven unto men" (Matthew 12:31). If the Lord is so gracious and kind, we must be also. (Spencer W. Kimball, "The Power of Forgiveness," *Ensign*, Nov. 1977, 48)

Peacemakers

Peacemakers shall be called the children of God. The trouble-maker, the striker against law and order, the leader of the mob, the law-breaker are prompted by motives of evil; and unless they desist, they will be known as the children of Satan rather than God. Withhold yourselves from him who would cause disquieting doubts by making light of sacred things, for he seeks not for peace but to spread confusion. That one who is quarrelsome or contentious, and whose arguments are for other purposes than to resolve the truth, is violating a fundamental principle laid down by the Master as an essential in the building of a full rich life. "Peace and goodwill to men on earth" was the angel song that heralded the birth of the Prince of Peace. (Harold B. Lee, *Stand Ye in Holy Places* [1974], 347)

Enduring Persecution Well

Enduring even includes the irony in which the worthy suffer for righteousness' sake: "Blessed are they which are persecuted for righteousness' sake: for theirs is the kingdom of heaven" (Matthew 5:10; italics added). And as for these times of terrorism, this counsel is given: "But and if ye suffer for righteousness' sake, happy are ye: and be not afraid of their terror, neither be troubled." (1 Peter 3:14; italics added)

Since "persecution ariseth because of the word," and since some then become offended (Matthew 13:21), enduring the indignity of being wronged for being right is yet another irony.Being misunderstood even when engaged in well-doing is part of it, too: "For it is better, if the will of God be so, that ye suffer for well doing, than for evil doing." (1 Peter 3:17) (Neal A. Maxwell, *We Will Prove Them Herewith* [1982], 116)

Our Heavenly Father Will Thank Us for Sharing His Gospel

I have said to many people when they have asked me, "What is there about this organization that you belong to? What is it that you are so concerned about, that you send missionaries all over the world?" I have replied sometimes, "We want you all to be happy. We want you all to rejoice as we rejoice. After awhile we will have to meet our record, and if we have been faithful, I am sure the Father of us all in the world will thank us and bless us for bringing so many of his sons and daughters to an understanding of the purpose of life and how to enjoy it under the influence of his Spirit." (George Albert Smith, *The Teachings of George Albert Smith* [1996], 165)

Light of the World

The light in your countenance comes because you have made and kept covenants with our Heavenly Father and His Son, Jesus Christ, and you have made choices which qualify you to have the companionship of the Holy Ghost. . . . By the way you live the gospel, you reflect His light. Your example will have a powerful effect for good on the earth. "Arise and shine forth, that thy light may be a standard for the nations" is a call to each of you. It is a call to move to higher ground. It is a call to leadership—to lead out in decency, purity, modesty, and holiness. It is a call to share this light with others. It is time to "arise and shine forth." (Elaine S. Dalton "It Shows in Your Face," *Ensign*, May 2006)

Learn to Love

That was it, the new commandment, "Thou shalt love.'" Love with all of your hearts. Love God and His children, wherever they might be and however they might treat you. How you are treated is of little consequence; the important thing is to learn to love everyone. Can we really love sinners? It seems to me that that is one of the requirements for our eternal progression. If we expect to be where the Gods are today, and they have love for all mankind—sinners as well as Saints—then certainly if we aspire to such a height, we must learn to love sinners as well as Saints, dark-skinned people as well as white, foreign tongues as well as our own native tongues. (John H. Groberg, *In the Eye of the Storm* [1993], 277–78)

Becoming Christlike

It is the simple Gospel of the Lord Jesus Christ, which teaches mankind to be true brethren and sisters, to love our neighbors as ourselves, to go the extra mile, to turn the other cheek, to forgive—even seventy times seven—to do unto others as we would be done by, to seek reconciliation wherein we have offended others, to avoid judging others, that we ourselves may not be judged; to be kind, patient, long-suffering, charitable, temperate, humble and God-like. (Mark E. Petersen, *The Way to Peace* [1969], 24)

Ask and It Will Be Given

The principle of asking is an eternal principle and law upon which many blessings are predicated. You must practice the principle of asking.

"Do ye not remember the things which the Lord hath said?—If ye will not harden your hearts, and ask me in faith, believing that ye shall receive, with diligence in keeping my commandments, surely these things shall be made known unto you." (1 Nephi 15:11)

"And whatsoever ye shall ask the Father in my name, which is right, believing that ye shall receive, behold it shall be given unto you." (3 Nephi 18:20)

"Therefore, ask, and ye shall receive; knock, and it shall be opened unto you; for he that asketh, receiveth; and unto him that knocketh, it shall be opened." (3 Nephi 27:29)

"And, as it is written—Whatsoever ye shall ask in faith, being united in prayer according to my command, ye shall receive." (D&C 29:6)

The Lord Will Provide the Way

Nephi went forth determined to do the Lord's will, even though he did not know exactly how to do it. Right after that, the Lord began to reveal to Nephi almost exactly what should be done. And, finally, he was able to obtain the plates. . . .

You are in the same position as Nephi was. As you go forward in faith, the Lord will reveal his will to you so that you will know what you should do. I have been greatly moved to see the amount of revelation that the Lord has poured out upon the members of his church about how to do his work and solve their problems, just as Nephi had revelation poured out upon him. (Gene R. Cook, *Living by the Power of Faith* [1985], 51)

The Missionary Spirit

"I know that which the Lord hath commanded me, and I glory in it. I do not glory of myself, but I glory in that which the Lord hath commanded me; yea, and this is my glory, that perhaps I may be an instrument in the hands of God to bring some soul to repentance; and this is my joy.

And behold, when I see many of my brethren truly penitent, and coming to the Lord their God, then is my soul filled with joy; then do I remember what the Lord has done for me, yea, even that he hath heard my prayer; yea, then do I remember his merciful arm which he extended towards me." (Alma 29:9–10)

The Source of Happiness

Whence comes your enjoyment? Whence come the glorious feelings that you have when you feel the best? Do they come from the outside? Do external circumstances produce real happiness of the kind that I describe? Doubtless, they contribute to happiness; but the purest joy, the greatest happiness, that which is most heavenly proceeds from within. A man must carry the principles of happiness and the love of God in his own breast, or he will not be happy.

It is not true enjoyment when it comes from any other source. Not from without, therefore, must we expect happiness and exaltation but from within. Deity is within us, and its development brings happiness and joy inexpressible. (George Q. Cannon, *Gospel*

Truth: Discourses and Writings of President George Q. Cannon, ed. Jerreld L. Newquist [1957], 78)

The Power of Pondering

President [Joseph F.] Smith said, "As I pondered over these things which are written [1 Peter 3–4], the eyes of my understanding were opened, and the Spirit of the Lord rested upon me, and I saw the hosts of the dead, both small and great." (D&C 138:11)

Such experiences are patterns that show us there is understanding and new knowledge to be gained when we search, pray, ponder, and meditate upon the holy scriptures and hear the voice of the Lord through his Spirit. In this way we come to know not only the doctrines of the gospel and the will of the Lord as revealed in ancient time but also the application to us individually in our own time. (Richard J. Matthews, in *The Prophet Joseph: Essays on the Life and Mission of Joseph Smith,* ed. Larry C. Porter and Susan Easton Black [1988], 183)

Prayer and Study

In relation, again, to these elders, I will tell you the first thing I used to do when I went preaching, particularly when I went to a fresh place—and that was to go aside to some place, anywhere I could get, into a field, a barn, into the woods, or my closet, and ask God to bless me and give me wisdom to meet all the circumstances with which I might have to contend; and the Lord gave me the wisdom I needed and sustained me. If you pursue a course of this kind, he will bless you also. Do not trust in yourselves, but study the best books—the Bible and Book of Mormon—and get all the information you can, and then cleave to God and keep yourselves free from corruption and pollution of every kind, and the blessings of the Most High will be with you. (John Taylor, *The Gospel Kingdom: Selections from the Writings and Discourses of John Taylor*, ed. G. Homer Durham [1943], 240)

There Is Power in the Book of Mormon

We have also inherited the Book of Mormon. If we live according to the principles taught in this inspired record, we will find happiness, strength, and exaltation. It was written for our day and for our problems. It addresses the challenges we face in today's world and will give us additional power to combat the adversary only if we will study and pray to understand its teachings and live by them. (Joseph B. Wirthlin, *Finding Peace in Our Lives* [1995], 140)

There is a power in the book which will begin to flow into your lives the moment you begin a serious study of the book. You will find greater power to resist temptation. You will find the power to avoid deception. You will find the power to stay on the strait and narrow path. The scriptures are called "the words of life" (D&C 84:85), and nowhere is that more true than it is of the Book of Mormon. When you begin to hunger and thirst after those words, you will find life in greater and greater abundance. (Ezra Taft Benson, "The Book of Mormon—Keystone of Our Religion," *Ensign*, Nov. 1986, 4)

The Infinite Sacrifice

The sacrifice of the Father's firstborn in the spirit, His Only Begotten Son in the flesh, was the sacrifice of a Creator—God. The Atoner was the Lord God Omnipotent, who created this and other planets (see D&C 76:24; Moses 1:33; Mosiah 3:5). Therefore, unlike any sacrifice a mortal could have made, Christ's was an infinite atonement made possible, declared King Benjamin, by the infinite goodness and mercy of God and by His willingness to see His Son suffer and be slain. (see Mosiah 4:6; 2 Nephi 9:7; Alma 34:10, 12; Mosiah 5:3) (Neal A. Maxwell, *Men and Women of Christ* [1991], 34)

God Knoweth All Things

An understanding that God knows all things, and that there is nothing which he does not know, is essentially necessary for man to have in order to exercise faith and gain salvation. As the Prophet said: "Without the knowledge of all things God would not be able to save any portion of his creatures; for it is by reason of the knowledge which he has of all things, from the beginning to the end, that enables him to give that understanding to his creatures by which they are made partakers of eternal life; and if it were not for the idea existing in the minds of men that God had all knowledge it would be impossible for them to exercise faith in him" (*Lectures on Faith*, 44). Not only does the Father know all things, but so likewise does the Son (D&C 38:2; 93:26), and the Holy Ghost. (D&C 35:19; 42:17) (Bruce R. McConkie, *Mormon Doctrine*, 2nd ed. [1966], 425)

Building Up the Kingdom of God

It will be necessary for the Saints to hearken to counsel and turn their attention to the Church, the establishment of the Kingdom, and lay aside every selfish principle, everything low and groveling; and stand forward in the cause of truth, and assist to the utmost of their power, those to whom has been given the pattern and design. Like those who held up the hands of Moses, so let us hold up the hands of those who are appointed to direct the affairs of the Kingdom, so that they may be strengthened, and be enabled to prosecute their great designs, and be instrumental in effecting the great work of the last days. (Joseph Smith, in *History of the Church*, 4:186)

Seek the Treasures of Heaven

And so, I would like to leave with you this thought, this message, that you will seek after the treasures of the Spirit, seek after the riches of goodness and mercy and righteous living. Go always after those things which are good. Follow along as you have been doing, seeking the finer cultural things of life. Discard the dross, cast it aside, trample it underfoot; cherish always and guard that which is beautiful in your lives. (J. Reuben Clark, Jr., *Behold the Lamb of God* [1991], 338)

Submit to the Will of God

If we want to be good, faithful Latter-day Saints, we have got to be willing to submit to the will of God in all things. We must feel as was once exclaimed on a certain occasion by the ancient Israelites, "The Lord shall be our Judge, the Lord shall be our King, the Lord shall be our Ruler, and he shall rule over us." That is the way I figure up these things; and if this was not so I would not give anything for our religion, or our religious ideas. I do not think that any of us can regulate, manage or conduct any of these matters, unless God be with us. And I will tell you another thing, God will not be with us unless we are one. (John Taylor, in *Journal of Discourses*, 18:283)

Recognize That God Is the Giver of All Things

The prayerful and humble man will always realize and feel that he is dependent upon the Lord for every blessing that he enjoys, and in praying to God he will not only pray for the light and the inspiration of His Holy Spirit to guide him, but he will feel to thank Him for the blessings that he receives, realizing that life, that health, that strength, and that all the intelligence which he possesses comes from God, who is the Author of his existence. (Heber J. Grant, *Improvement Era*, Dec. 1942, 779)

The Lord Loves Us

He doeth not anything save it be for the benefit of the world; for he loveth the world, even that he layeth down his own life that he may draw all men unto him. Wherefore, he commandeth none that they shall not partake of his salvation. (2 Nephi 26:24)

The Savior spoke prophetically of that sacrifice and of the love that culminated in his redemptive sacrifice when he declared, "Greater love hath no man than this, that a man lay down his life for his friends." (John 15:13)

To all of us who would be his disciples, he has given the great commandment, "A new commandment I give unto you, That ye love one another; as I have loved you, that ye also love one another." (John

13:34) (Gordon B. Hinckley, *Faith: The Essence of True Religion* [1989], 48)

Disciples Are Led by the Holy Spirit

After all, as Alma said, discipleship means being "led by the Holy Spirit, becoming humble, meek, submissive, patient, full of love, and all long-suffering" (Alma 13:28). Moreover, the companion plea is that "ye should be humble, and be submissive and gentle; easy to be entreated; full of patience and long-suffering; being temperate in all things" (Alma 7:23). Being easy to be entreated requires intellectual humility. This is at obvious odds with the styles and panache of the world. (Neal A. Maxwell, *Not My Will, But Thine* [1998], 105)

We Are Enabled by the Infinite Atonement

By grace, the Savior accomplished His atoning sacrifice so that all mankind will attain immortality. By His grace, and by our faith in His atonement and repentance of our sins, we receive the strength to do the works necessary that we otherwise could not do by our own power. By His grace we receive an endowment of blessing and spiritual strength that may eventually lead us to eternal life if we endure to the end. By His grace we become more like His divine personality. Yes, it is "by grace that we are saved, after all we can do" (2 Nephi 25:23). (Ezra Taft Benson, *The Teachings of Ezra Taft Benson* [1988], 35–54)

The Holy Ghost Will Show Us All Things to Do

May we through worship, meditation, communion, and reverence sense the reality of being able to have a close relationship with our Father in heaven. I bear you my testimony that it is real; that we can commune with our Heavenly Father, and if we so live to be worthy of the companionship of the Holy Spirit, he will guide us into all truth; he will show us things to come; he will bring all things to our remembrance; he will testify of the divinity of the Lord Jesus Christ and of the restoration of the gospel. (David O. McKay, *Man May Know for Himself: Teachings of President David O. McKay*, comp. Clare Middlemiss [1967], 28)

Magnify Your Calling

We magnify our priesthood and enlarge our calling when we serve with diligence and enthusiasm in those responsibilities to which we are called by proper authority. I emphasize the words, "diligence and enthusiasm." This work has not reached its present stature through indifference on the part of those who have labored in its behalf. The Lord needs men, both young and old, who will carry the banners of His kingdom with positive strength and determined purpose. . . .

We magnify our calling, we enlarge the potential of our priesthood when we reach out to those in distress and give strength to those who falter. (Gordon B. Hinckley, *Teachings of Gordon B. Hinckley* [1997], 478–79)

You Need the Spirit

I am satisfied that the most effective means each of us has in our calling to share the gospel is the Spirit of the Lord. . . .

Truly we are engaged in a marvelous work and a wonder. . . .

One cannot think of the hundreds of millions who have never heard of this work without wondering how our charge to teach all mankind can ever be accomplished. . . . As we put forth our effort and pray humbly for inspiration, we will be blessed in our desires to share the gospel with our families, friends, neighbors, and acquaintances. (Gordon B. Hinckley, *Faith: The Essence of True Religion* [1989], 55)

The Prophet Speaks for God

Gratefully, we follow prophets who have been given a divine commission: "Whatsoever they shall speak when moved upon by the Holy Ghost shall be scripture, shall be the will of the Lord, shall be the mind of the Lord, shall be the word of the Lord, shall be the voice of the Lord, and the power of God unto salvation."

While we follow prophetic teachings, we can develop our spiritual capacities by emulating one such as President Gordon B. Hinckley. I thank God for this prophet. He is the Lord's anointed. Willingly I follow him. I love him and sustain him. (Russell M. Nelson, *Perfection Pending, and Other Favorite Discourses* [1998], 17–18)

Keep the Faith—Be Happy

Keep the faith. Your happiness lies in following the gospel of Jesus Christ. That's the case with all of us. "Wickedness never was happiness" (Alma 41:10), said Alma to his son Corianton. That's as true as the sunrise in the morning. "Wickedness never was happiness." There is no happiness in doing what's wrong. There is no happiness in sin. There is misery and pain and regret and heartache and suffering. Happiness lies in walking in righteousness. Happiness lies in faithfulness and in righteousness. (Gordon B. Hinckley, *Teachings of Gordon B. Hinckley* [1997], 256)

Repentance Is the Key to Peace

If sin has deprived us of peace within, we can repent and seek forgiveness. The Lord said that he "cannot look upon sin with the least degree of allowance; nevertheless, he that repents and does the commandments of the Lord shall be forgiven" (D&C 1:31–32). President Spencer W. Kimball wrote: "The essence of the miracle of forgiveness is that it brings peace to the previously anxious, restless, frustrated, perhaps tormented soul. In a world of turmoil and contention this is indeed a priceless gift." (Joseph B. Wirthlin, *Finding Peace in Our Lives* [1995], 9)

Remembering the Goodness of God

How can you and I remember, always, the goodness of God, that we can retain a remission of our sins? The Apostle John recorded what the Savior taught us of a gift of remembrance which comes through the gift of the Holy Ghost: "But the Comforter, which is the Holy Ghost, whom the Father will send in my name, he shall teach you all things, and bring all things to your remembrance, whatsoever I have said unto you." (John 14:26)

The Holy Ghost brings back memories of what God has taught us. And one of the ways God teaches us is with his blessings; and so, if we choose to exercise faith, the Holy Ghost will bring God's kindnesses to our remembrance. (Henry B. Eyring, *To Draw Closer to God: A Collection of Discourses* [1997], 77–78)

Repent or Suffer

Under the law and justice of God, sinners *are* punished. We believe that men will be punished for their own sins (Article of Faith Two). Through the prophet Isaiah, the Lord said he would "punish the inhabitants of the earth for their iniquity" (Isaiah

26:21). God's law could not exist "save there was a punishment" (Alma 42:17). There is "a punishment affixed" for every sin (Alma 42:18; also see Amos 3:1–2). Amulek explained that "he that exercises no faith unto repentance is exposed to the whole law of the demands of justice" (Alma 34:16). Justice requires that the *unrepentant* sinner suffer for his own sins. "If they would not repent," the Savior said, "they must suffer even as I." (D&C 19:17) (Dallin H. Oaks, *The Lord's Way* [1991], 222)

The Learner Needs to Be Receptive to Learn

And when the priests left their labor to impart the word of God unto the people, the people also left their labors to hear the word of God. And when the priest had imparted unto them the word of God they all returned again diligently unto their labors; and the priest, not esteeming himself above his hearers, for the preacher was no better than the hearer, neither was the teacher any better than the learner; and thus they were all equal, and they did all labor, every man according to his strength. (Alma 1:26)

Whether the classroom is a seat on the plane, a hotel room, a home, a chapel, the Mission Training

Center, the Salt Lake Tabernacle, or a satellite audience, reverence and a receptive heart must be present if this teacher is to teach and the learner learn. (Lucile C. Tate, *Boyd K. Packer: A Watchman on the Tower* [1995], 278)

Remember the Goodness of God

The prophets labor diligently that they might persuade their people "to come unto Christ, and partake of the goodness of God, that they might enter into his rest" (Jacob 1:7). If we but repent and do not harden our hearts, we may through our faithfulness likewise enter into that rest and glory of the Lord (see Alma 12:34). Moroni has exhorted us to remember the mercies of the Lord: "Behold, I would exhort you that when ye shall read these things, if it be wisdom in God that ye should read them, that ye would remember how merciful the Lord hath been unto the children of men, from the creation of Adam even down until the time that ye shall receive these things, and ponder it in your hearts." (Moroni 10:3)

What We Are Will Rise with Us in the Resurrection

The spirit and the body shall be reunited again in its perfect form; both limb and joint shall be restored to its proper frame, even as we now are at this time; and we shall be brought to stand before God, knowing even as we know now, and have a bright recollection of all our guilt. (Alma 11:43)

Let us live with the certain knowledge that some day "we shall be brought to stand before God, knowing even as we know now, and have a bright recollection of all our guilt" (Alma 11:43). Let us live today knowing that we shall live forever. Let us live with the conviction that whatever principle of intelligence and beauty and truth and goodness we make a part of our life here, it will rise with us in the resurrection. (Gordon B. Hinckley, *Teachings of Gordon B. Hinckley*, [1997], 173)

Blessings Await the Faithful

Knowingly we wanted the risks of mortality, which would allow the exercise of agency and accountability. "This life [was to become] a probationary state;

a time to prepare to meet God." But we regarded the returning home as the best part of that long-awaited trip, just as we do now. Before embarking on any journey, we like to have some assurance of a round-trip ticket. Returning from earth to life in our heavenly home requires passage through—and not around—the doors of death. We were born to die, and we die to live. As seedlings of God, we barely blossom on earth; we fully flower in heaven. (Russell M. Nelson, *Perfection Pending, and Other Favorite Discourses* [1998], 137)

Forsake the World for the Lord's Sake

As we hear the Lord's answers, they are not always easy to bear. For example, Jesus' discourse on the dangers of wealth produced anxiety and inquiry among His followers: "When his disciples heard it, they were exceedingly amazed, saying, Who then can be saved?" (Matthew 19:25). Note the Savior's response as rendered by the Joseph Smith Translation: "But Jesus beheld their thoughts, and said unto them, With men this is impossible; but if they will forsake all things for my sake, with God whatsoever things I speak are possible" (JST, Matthew 19:26). We can succeed, if we will forsake the world. Otherwise the soul-stretching, mind-expanding demands of the gospel would be impossible to meet. To have one's soul "greatly enlarge[d] without hypocrisy" (D&C 121:42) is part of the journey of discipleship. Perhaps no question was more terse while eliciting more magnificent though brief responses than when God the Father said of His plan of salvation and of the need for a Savior, "Whom shall I send?" "Here am I, send me" (Abraham 3:27). The rest is supernal history! (Neal A. Maxwell, *Men and Women of Christ* [1991], 124)

Study and Ponder the Scriptures

There are special gifts and endowments reserved for those who study and ponder the scriptures; for those who treasure up the Lord's word; for those who fast and pray and seek knowledge by the power of the Spirit. They receive guidance and enlightenment that can be gained in no other way. They become men of sound understanding. They gain the spirit of revelation and of prophecy and teach and speak with power from on high. (Marion G. Romney, *Learning for the Eternities* [1977], ii)

Teach with Power

The greatest challenge we have today is to teach the members of this church to keep the commandments of God. Never before has there been such a challenge to the doctrine of righteousness and purity and chastity. The moral standards are being eroded by powers of evil. There is nothing more important for us to do than to teach as powerfully, led by the Spirit of the Lord, as we can in order to persuade our people in the world to live close to the Lord in this hour of great temptation. (Harold B. Lee, *The Teachings of Harold B. Lee*, ed. Clyde J. Williams [1996], 85)

Gratitude Is the Catalyst for Change

King Benjamin's teaching had a miraculous effect. Gratitude for what they had led to faith unto repentance. That led to forgiveness. That produced new gratitude. And then King Benjamin taught that, if we can remember and so remain grateful, we will retain a remission of our sins through all the losses and the gains of life. (Henry B. Eyring, "Remembrance and Gratitude," *Ensign*, Nov. 1989, 11)

In the Strength of the Lord

But Ammon said unto him: I do not boast in my own strength, nor in my own wisdom; but behold, my joy is full, yea, my heart is brim with joy, and I will rejoice in my God.

Yea, I know that I am nothing; as to my strength I am weak; therefore I will not boast of myself, but I will boast of my God, for in his strength I can do all things; yea, behold, many mighty miracles we have wrought in this land, for which we will praise his name forever. (Alma 26:11–12)

I will go where the Lord and the leaders of His Church want me to go, I will do what they want me to do, I will teach what they want me to teach, and I will strive to become what I should and must become. In the strength of the Lord and through His grace, I know that you and I can be blessed to accomplish all things. (David A. Bednar, "In the Strength of the Lord," *Ensign*, Nov. 2004, 76)

Learn by Faith

In the scriptures, the Lord has specified how we learn by faith. We must be humble, cultivate faith, repent of our sins, serve our fellowmen, and keep the commandments of God (see Ether 12:27; D&C 1:28; D&C 12:8; D&C 50:28; D&C 63:23; D&C 136:32–33). As the Book of Mormon says, "Yea, he that repenteth and exerciseth faith, and bringeth forth good works, and prayeth continually without ceasing—unto such it is given to know the mysteries of God. (Alma 26:22) (Dallin H. Oaks, "Alternate Voices," *Ensign*, May 1989, 27)

Plead with Members to Help

The answer has been given by a Prophet of God. Every member of The Church of Jesus Christ of Latter-day Saints should be a missionary. Each member should bring one or more of his neighbors and friends into the Church each year. Each member must increase his faith and turn up his divine luster and candle power and let his light so shine before men that they may see his good works, and glorify their Father which is in heaven. (Matthew 5:16) (Bernard P. Brockbank, in Conference Report, Oct. 1966, 89)

The Worth of Souls

This is God's work. He wants us to participate with Him and His Beloved Son in bringing the gospel into the lives of all of His children. The Lord has promised us that our joy will be great if we bring just one soul unto Him (see D&C 18:15–16). Let us exercise greater faith and work together, members and missionaries, to bring many more souls unto Him. Let every family in the Church include as part of their daily family prayers a plea with the Lord to go before your family members and help them to find someone prepared to receive the message of the restored gospel of Jesus Christ. (M. Russell Ballard, "Now Is the Time," *Ensign*, Nov. 2000, 75)

True Conversion Leads to Caring for Others

The scriptures confirm that the truly converted do more than just forsake the enticements of the world. They love God and their fellowmen. Their minds and hearts are centered on the Savior's atoning sacrifice. From the moment of their respective conversions, Enos, Alma the Younger, Paul, and others turned wholeheartedly to the task of bringing themselves and their fellowmen to God. Worldly power and possessions lost their former significance. The sons of Mosiah refused an earthly kingdom and risked their lives for the sake of others. These faithful sons were driven by the hope that they might be able to help save even one soul—thus winning for themselves and their brethren a place in God's eternal kingdom. (Robert D. Hales, "The Covenant of Baptism: To Be in the Kingdom and of the Kingdom," *Ensign*, Nov. 2000, 6)

The Glory and Joy of Missionary Work

I know that which the Lord hath commanded me, and I glory in it. I do not glory of myself, but I glory in that which the Lord hath commanded me; yea, and this is my glory, that perhaps I may be an instrument in the hands of God to bring some soul to repentance; and this is my joy.

And behold, when I see many of my brethren truly penitent, and coming to the Lord their God, then is my soul filled with joy; then do I remember what the Lord has done for me, yea, even that he hath heard my prayer; yea, then do I remember his merciful arm which he extended towards me. (Alma 29:9–10)

Brethren and sisters, in serving the Lord we reap everlasting joy. We are not striving for the praise of men, but for the praise and honor that comes from God only. (Charles A. Callis, in Conference Report, Oct. 1910, 74)

Find Joy in the Success of Others

Said Alma: "I do not joy in my own success alone, but my joy is more full because of the success of my brethren. . . .

Behold, they have labored exceedingly, and have brought forth much fruit; and how great shall be their reward! . . .

Now, when I think of the success of these my brethren . . . great is my joy." (Alma 29:14–16)

Look for the good in others and learn. Give sincere credit where credit is due. Spend less time fault-finding and more time identifying strengths. Yes, try to catch others doing good! Don't put a stumbling block before others; instead, give them a step upward in the form of a recognized success. (See Romans 14:13) (Carlos E. Asay, *In the Lord's Service: A Guide to Spiritual Development* [1990], 95)

Judging Between Christ and Anti-Christ

Korihor tried to teach people that there is happiness and joy to be found outside of God and the gospel. The Book of Mormon clearly shows that this is not true. It reminds us of the power of God's word, the power to change our lives, the power to bring us peace and joy and the answers to those issues in life that trouble us. As we learn this lesson from Korihor, we again are reminded of the promise of President Ezra Taft Benson, the living Prophet:

"I bless you with increased discernment to judge between Christ and anti-Christ. I bless you with increased power to do good and resist evil. I bless you with increased understanding of the Book of Mormon. I promise you that from this moment forward, if we will daily sup from its pages and abide by its precepts, God will pour out upon each child of Zion and the Church a blessing hitherto unknown." (Gerald N. Lund, *Selected Writings of Gerald N. Lund: Gospel Scholars Series* [1999], 132)

Christ Is the Gospel

Each time Jesus or His prophets say "This is my gospel," the brief declaration implies a loving Heavenly Father who has sent His Only Begotten Son to rescue and redeem mankind. . . . Yet some people reject this simple truth, seeking instead things they cannot understand. Theirs is a mistake of reckoning involving more than a few degrees on life's compass. It is an enormous error resulting from "looking beyond the mark" (Jacob 4:14)—the mark of Christ, who is at the center of it all. (Neal A. Maxwell, *Not My Will, But Thine* [1998], 7)

The Nephite Cycle

Most of us seem to have the "Nephite cycle" as part of our character. There is a point when we are teachable; our humility enables us to grow and to ride the crest of spirituality. Then there are other times when we begin to feel self-sufficient and puffed up with pride. These times cause us to fall of our own weight and ill-doing into pits of spiritual darkness. How much better it would be if we kept in remembrance our God and our religion and broke the cycle by consistent worship and righteous living. How much better it would be if we were humbled by the word of the Lord and strong enough in spirit to remember our God in whatsoever circumstances we find ourselves (see Alma 32:12–25). (Carlos E. Asay, *Family Pecan Trees: Planting a Legacy of Faith at Home* [1992], 194)

Start Now—Don't Procrastinate

The same power of an early choice to exercise faith and to be persistent in obedience applies to gaining the faith to resist temptation and to gain forgiveness. The best time to resist temptation is early. The best time to repent is now. The enemy of our souls will place thoughts in our minds to tempt us. We can decide early to exercise faith, to cast out evil thoughts before we act on them. And we can choose quickly to repent when we do sin, before Satan can weaken our faith and bind us. Seeking forgiveness is always better now than later. (Henry B. Eyring, in Conference Report, Oct. 2005)

Experiment upon the Word

We know that both members and nonmembers are more likely to be thoroughly converted to the gospel of Jesus Christ when there is a willingness to experiment upon the word (see Alma 32:27). This is an attitude of both mind and heart that includes a desire to know the truth and a willingness to act on that desire. For those investigating the Church, the experiment can be as simple as agreeing to read the

Book of Mormon, to pray about it, and to earnestly seek to know if Joseph Smith was the Lord's prophet.

True conversion comes through the power of the Spirit. . . . These experiences with the Spirit follow naturally when a person is willing to experiment upon the word. This is how we come to *feel* the gospel is true. (M. Russell Ballard, "Now Is the Time," *Ensign*, Nov. 2000, 75)

Knowledge by Faith

Learning by faith is not easy. To one schooled in the doctrines of salvation and the history of the Restoration and with a testimony of the divine origin of this church, we would remind you that the acquiring of knowledge by faith is no easy road to learning. It demands strenuous effort and a continual striving by faith.

In short, learning by faith is no task for a lazy man. Someone has said, in effect, that such a process requires the bending of the whole soul, the calling up from the depths of the human mind and linking it with God—the right connection must be formed. Then only comes "knowledge by faith." (Harold B. Lee, *The Teachings of Harold B. Lee*, ed. Clyde J. Williams, 331)

Knowing God

The Lord cannot always be known by the thunder of His voice, by the display of His glory or by the manifestation of His power. . . .

We would say . . . seek to know God in your closets, call upon him in the fields. Follow the directions of the Book of Mormon, and pray over, and for your families, your cattle, your flocks, your herds, your corn, and all things that you possess; ask the blessing of God upon all your labors, and everything that you engage in. Be virtuous and pure; be men of integrity and truth; keep the commandments of God; and then you will be able more perfectly to understand the difference between right and wrong—between the things of God and the things of men; and your path will be like that of the just, which shineth brighter and brighter unto the perfect day. (Joseph Smith, *Teachings of the Prophet Joseph Smith*, comp. Joseph Fielding Smith [1938], 247)

Pray to Overcome Temptation

We should pray much, that we may not be overcome by temptation, and that we may have power to contend against every principle in the earth that is not ordained of God. We ought to seek for strength and ability to live and to prevail against every evil, in order that the truth may triumph, and salvation, immortality and eternal life be brought to light through our efforts and labors, as they were through the efforts and labors of the Savior and His early disciples. (Franklin D. Richards, *Millennial Star*, Dec. 1897, 774)

Conversion Leads to Service

How do we know if we are truly converted? Self-examination tests are available in the scriptures. One measures the degree of conversion prerequisite to baptism. Another measures our willingness to serve others. To His disciple Peter, the Lord said, "I have prayed for thee, that thy faith fail not: and when thou art converted, strengthen thy brethren" [Luke 22:32]. Willingness to serve and strengthen others stands as a symbol of one's readiness to be healed. (Russell M. Nelson, "Jesus Christ—the Master Healer," in Conference Report, Oct. 2005)

Feasting on the Word

Since feasting on the word of God has a "more powerful effect upon the minds of the people than

. . . anything else" (Alma 31:5), the more of the word of God we have and act upon, the more we will press forward. Much spiritual energy is necessary for the marathon of discipleship.

As a great blessing, the word of God has been richly given to us in the Restoration. It provides a full and firm basis for real faith, especially in a world in which many are struggling to believe, and still others, bereft of a fresh view, have simply quit struggling! (Neal A. Maxwell, *A Wonderful Flood of Light* [1990], 11)

Trust in the Lord

I know, as did Alma of old, that "whosoever shall put their trust in God shall be supported in their trials, and their troubles, and their afflictions, and shall be lifted up at the last day."

Our Heavenly Father is a powerful, moving, directing being. While we may, at times, bear burdens of sorrow, pain, and grief; while we may struggle to understand trials of faith we are called to pass through; while life may seem dark and dreary—through faith, we have absolute confidence that a loving Heavenly Father is at our side. (Joseph B. Wirthlin, "Shall He Find Faith on the Earth?" *Ensign*, Nov. 2002, 82)

You Are the Messengers of the Restoration

As another important phase of "a marvelous work and a wonder," the Prophet was commanded that he and the Church members should take the gospel and the Book of Mormon to every nation, kindred, tongue, and people, searching out the honest in heart, in order that all of the covenants that had been made with Abraham, Isaac, and Jacob and others of the house of Israel might be fulfilled. Thus through this missionary work, Christ would fulfil his covenants which he had made with the children of men by sending his messengers throughout the earth, declaring the restoration of the gospel and proclaiming Jesus to be the Christ, the only name given under heaven whereby man can be saved. (Milton R. Hunter, in Conference Report, Oct. 1958, 29)

Messengers of the Gospel of Jesus Christ

"And then shall they say: How beautiful upon the mountains are the feet of him that bringeth good tidings unto them, that publisheth peace; that bringeth good tidings unto them of good, that publisheth salvation; that saith unto Zion: Thy God reigneth!" [3 Nephi 20:40]

These familiar passages, written first by Isaiah but spoken of and inspired by Jehovah himself, are often applied to anyone—especially missionaries—who bring the good tidings of the gospel and publish peace to the souls of men. . . . This psalm of appreciation applies specifically to Christ. It is he and only he who ultimately brings the good tidings of salvation. Only through him is true, lasting peace published. (Jeffrey R. Holland, *Christ and the New Covenant: The Messianic Message of the Book of Mormon* [1997], 286)

Preach the Gospel

Some may wonder why General Authorities speak of the same things from conference to conference. As I study the utterances of the prophets through the centuries, their pattern is very clear. We seek, in the words of Alma, to teach people "an everlasting hatred against sin and iniquity." We preach "repentance, and faith on the Lord Jesus Christ" (Alma 37:32, 33). We praise humility. We seek to teach people "to withstand every temptation of the devil, with their faith on the Lord Jesus Christ" (Alma 37:33). We teach our people "to never be weary of good works." (Alma 37:34) (Spencer W.

Kimball, "The Stone Cut without Hands," *Ensign*, May 1976, 4)

Miracles Are Wrought through Faith and Righteousness

Faith and righteousness are the powers by which miracles are wrought (2 Nephi 26:13; Mosiah 8:18), and miracles are not manifest until after the foundation of faith has been securely built (Ether 12:15–16, 18). Miracles cease when wickedness prevails among a people (Mormon 1:13); their absence is thus conclusive proof of the apostate status of any church or people. "There was not any man who could do a miracle in the name of Jesus," the Nephite record states, "save he were cleansed every whit from his iniquity." (3 Nephi 8:1) (Bruce R. McConkie, *Mormon Doctrine*, 2nd ed. [1966], 507)

Beware of Pride

In an early revelation the Lord warned Oliver: "Behold, thou art blessed, and art under no condemnation. But beware of pride, lest thou shouldst enter into temptation." Oliver had great intellect and enjoyed marvelous spiritual blessings. However, over time he forgot the Lord's warning, and pride entered into his heart. Brigham Young later said of this pride: "I have seen men who belonged to this kingdom, and who really thought that if they were not associated with it, it could not progress." (James E. Faust, "The Prophetic Voice," *Ensign*, May 1996, 4)

Blessings of Righteousness

> And then shall it come to pass, that the spirits of those who are righteous are received into a state of happiness, which is called paradise, a state of rest, a state of peace, where they shall rest from all their troubles and from all care, and sorrow. (Alma 40:12)

This knowledge is one of the greatest incentives that we have to live right in this life, to pass through mortality, doing and feeling and accomplishing good. The spirits of all men, as soon as they depart from this mortal body, whether they are good or evil, we are told in the Book of Mormon, are taken home to that God who gave them life, where there is a separation, a partial judgment, and the spirits of those who are righteous are received into a state of happiness which is called paradise, a state of rest, a state of peace, where they expand in wisdom, where they have respite from all their troubles, and where care and sorrow do not annoy. (Joseph F. Smith, *Improvement Era*, 1904, 621)

Adversity Is Part of the Test

The words of Peter, Brigham Young, and in other scriptures, then, make clear that trials and adversities are not to be seen as a "strange thing" but are part of the normal pattern of life on earth. Mortality is a proving ground, a test of faith and obedience. By refining the submissive person, it makes him or her fit to return home to God. The course is not easy, but the grace of God is available to help us through it. And those who endure it well while clinging to the iron rod will receive the greatest of all gifts—eternal life. (Neal A. Maxwell, *If Thou Endure It Well* [1996], 10)

Judged by Our Works and the Desires of Our Heart

And it is requisite with the justice of God that men should be judged according to their works; and if their works were good in this life, and

> the desires of their hearts were good, that they should also, at the last day, be restored unto that which is good. (Alma 41:3)

Another unchanging principle, brothers and sisters, is that of your eventual judgment. Each of you will be judged according to your individual works and the desires of your hearts. You will not be required to pay the debt of any other. Your eventual placement in the celestial, terrestrial, or telestial kingdom will not be determined by chance. The Lord has prescribed unchanging requirements for each. You can know what the scriptures teach, and pattern your lives accordingly. (Russell M. Nelson, "Constancy amid Change," *Ensign*, Nov. 1993, 33)

Wickedness Never Was Happiness

> Do not suppose, because it has been spoken concerning restoration, that ye shall be restored from sin to happiness. Behold, I say unto you, wickedness never was happiness. (Alma 41:10)

It is not God who has given us the spirit of fear; this comes from the adversary. So many of us are fearful of what our peers will say, that we will be looked upon with disdain and criticized if we stand for what is right. But I remind you that "wickedness never was happiness" (Alma 41:10). Evil never was happiness. Sin never was happiness. Happiness lies in the power and the love and the sweet simplicity of the gospel of Jesus Christ. (Gordon B. Hinckley, "Converts and Young Men," *Ensign*, May 1997, 47)

Zion—The Pure in Heart

The gospel, in fact, gives us glimpses of the far horizon, revealing a glow from the lights of the City of God. It is a place of happy countenances, where justice and mercy as well as righteousness and truth are constant companions. Herein gentleness and generosity prevail, "without compulsory means" (D&C 121:46). Coarseness and selfishness are unknown, belonging to a previous and primitive place. Here envy would be a sure embarrassment. Neighbors are esteemed as self. This city, where all the residents keep the first and second great commandments, is a community of striking individuals of one heart and of one mind. (Neal A. Maxwell, "Called and Prepared from the Foundation of the World," *Ensign*, May 1986, 34)

Gratitude Brings Repentance

But God ceaseth not to be God, and mercy claimeth the penitent, and mercy cometh because of the atonement; and the atonement bringeth to pass the resurrection of the dead; and the resurrection of the dead bringeth back men into the presence of God; and thus they are restored into his presence, to be judged according to their works, according to the law and justice. (Alma 42:23)

Gratitude is also the foundation upon which repentance is built.

The Atonement brought mercy through repentance to balance justice. How thankful I am for the doctrine of repentance. Repentance is essential to salvation. We are mortal—we are not perfect—we will make mistakes. When we make mistakes and do not repent, we suffer. (Robert D. Hales, "Gratitude for the Goodness of God," *Ensign*, May 1992, 63)

Heed the Words of the Prophets

As people heed the words of the prophets, the Lord blesses them. When they disregard His word, however, distress and suffering often follow. Over and over, the Book of Mormon teaches this great lesson. In its pages we read of the ancient inhabitants of the American continent who, because of their righteousness, were blessed of the Lord and became prosperous. Yet often this prosperity turned into a curse in that it caused them to "harden their hearts, and . . . forget the Lord their God." (Joseph B. Wirthlin, "Journey to Higher Ground," Conference Report, Oct. 2005)

Be Your Best Self

To you men I issue a challenge. Run from the tide of sleaze that would overcome you. Flee the evils of the world. Be loyal to your better self. Be loyal to the best that is in you. Be faithful and true to the covenants that are associated with the priesthood of God. You cannot wallow about in lasciviousness, you cannot lie, you cannot cheat, you cannot take advantage of others in unrighteousness without denying that touch of divinity with which each of us came into this life. I would pray with all of my strength, brethren, that we would rise above it and be loyal to our best selves. (Gordon B. Hinckley, "Loyalty," *Ensign*, May 2003, 58)

Choose Who You Will Serve and How You Will Serve

> And if it seem evil unto you to serve the Lord, choose you this day whom ye will serve; whether the gods which your fathers served that were on the other side of the flood, or the gods of the Amorites, in whose land ye dwell: but as for me and my house, we will serve the Lord.
> (Joshua 24:15)

Joshua reminds us of the importance of making decisions promptly. . . . Not tomorrow, not when we get ready, not when it is convenient—but "this day," choose whom you will serve. He who invites us to follow will always be out in front of us with His Spirit and influence setting the pace. He has charted and marked the course, opened the gates, and shown the way. . . . We can best get on the course and stay on the course by doing as Jesus did—make a total commitment to do the will of His Father. (Marvin J. Ashton, *Be of Good Cheer* [1987], 56)

Take No Offense

We have not the right to hate any of the creatures of God, but we have been commanded to love them, and also to forgive them if they have offended us. I believe that you can put this down as a principle, that to start with there are very few offenders who willfully intend to offend, not having given full thought to their acts. They do something that offends us, and we at once feel offended and angry and, perhaps, we let it grow to that greater amount of anger that we call hatred. This should not be. Perhaps if we had spoken to our brother at once we would have learned that he did not really mean what we thought he did, and that we have become offended too hastily. Let us have enough charity for one another that we will not allow anything to be an offense to cause us hardness of heart. (Anthon H. Lund, in Conference Report, Oct. 1920, 13)

Power of the Word

Therefore, Helaman and his brethren went
forth, and did declare the word of God with
much power unto the convincing of many
people of their wickedness, which did cause

> them to repent of their sins and to be baptized unto the Lord their God. (Alma 62:45)

There is an interesting conceptual chain related to the "power of the word" that flows through this section of the Book of Mormon. As the account of the mission of the sons of Mosiah begins, Alma testifies that through personal preparation, including scripture study, fasting, and prayer, these brethren were able to teach the word "with power and authority of God" (Alma 17:3). Then, in the very next verse, Mormon notes that they had great success in bringing the Lamanites to the gospel because of "the power of their words" (Alma 17:4). (Gerald N. Lund, *Selected Writings of Gerald N. Lund: Gospel Scholars Series* [1999], 118)

Be Submissive to the Word

> Yea, we see that whosoever will may lay hold upon the word of God, which is quick and powerful, which shall divide asunder all the cunning and the snares and the wiles of the devil, and lead the man of Christ in a strait and narrow course across that everlasting gulf of misery which is prepared to engulf the wicked. (Helaman 3:29)

The spiritually submissive will make it through. The word of God will lead the man and the woman of Christ in a strait and narrow course across that everlasting gulf of misery (Hel. 3:29) and land their souls at the right hand of God in the kingdom of heaven, "to sit down with Abraham, Isaac, and Jacob, and the holy prophets who have been ever since the world began" (Alma 7:25; see also Ether 12:4). (Neal A. Maxwell, "For I Will Lead You Along," *Ensign*, May 1988, 7)

Seek Eternal Things

And now my sons, behold I have somewhat more to desire of you, which desire is, that ye may not do these things that ye may boast, but that ye may do these things to lay up for yourselves a treasure in heaven, yea, which is eternal, and which fadeth not away; yea, that ye may have that precious gift of eternal life, which we have reason to suppose hath been given to our fathers. (Helaman 5:8)

Nephi's example teaches us that the blessings of the scriptures are far more valuable than property and other worldly things. Pursuing the things of the world can sometimes give us momentary pleasures but not lasting joy and happiness. When we seek after the things of the Spirit, the rewards are eternal and will bring us the satisfaction we seek through this mortal experience. (L. Tom Perry, "Blessings Resulting from Reading the Book of Mormon," in Conference Report, Oct. 2005)

The Only Way to Be Saved

O remember, remember, my sons, the words which king Benjamin spake unto his people; yea, remember that there is no other way nor means whereby man can be saved, only through the atoning blood of Jesus Christ, who shall come; yea, remember that he cometh to redeem the world. (Helaman 5:9)

The truth was spoken by Nephi when he said, "We are saved [by grace], after all we can do" (2 Nephi 25:23).

It will require maximum effort for us to bring ourselves within the reach of the atoning blood of Jesus Christ so that we can be saved. There will be no government dole which can get us through the pearly gates. Nor will anyone go through those gates who wants to go through on the efforts of another. (Marion G. Romney, "Fundamental Welfare Services," *Ensign*, May 1979, 94)

Christ—The Sure Foundation

And now, my sons, remember, remember that it is upon the rock of our Redeemer, who is Christ, the Son of God, that ye must build your foundation; that when the devil shall send forth his mighty winds, yea, his shafts in the whirlwind, yea, when all his hail and his mighty storm shall beat upon you, it shall have no power over you to drag you down to the gulf of misery and endless wo, because of the rock upon which ye are built, which is a sure foundation, a foundation whereon if men build they cannot fall. (Helaman 5:12)

I pray, brothers and sisters, that all of us, especially those who are coming into manhood and womanhood, may give sober thought to these glorious principles and be able to build our lives upon the sure foundation of the gospel of Jesus Christ, "whereon if men build they cannot fall." (Elray L. Christiansen, in Conference Report, Apr. 1958, 37)

Whom the Lord Loveth He Chasteneth

Even when righteously chastised or rebuked, we need not faint, for in the correcting is renewing love: "My son, despise not thou the chastening of the Lord, nor faint when thou art rebuked of him:

For whom the Lord loveth he chasteneth." (Hebrews 12:5–8)

One's life, therefore, cannot be both faith-filled and stress-free. President Wilford Woodruff counseled us all about the mercy that is inherent in some adversity: "The chastisements we have had from time to time have been for our good, and are essential to learn wisdom, and carry us through a school of experience we never could have passed through without." (Neal A. Maxwell, "Lest Ye Be Wearied and Faint in Your Minds," *Ensign*, May 1991, 88)

Blessed Are They Who Repent

Therefore, blessed are they who will repent and hearken unto the voice of the Lord their God; for these are they that shall be saved.

And may God grant, in his great fulness, that men might be brought unto repentance and good works, that they might be restored unto grace for grace, according to their works.

And I would that all men might be saved." (Helaman 12:23–24)

That great truth ought to fill us all with hope, as long as we are quick to remember that the effect of grace in our lives is conditioned upon repenting of our sins.

"Therefore, blessed are they who will repent." . . .

A repentant heart and good works are the very conditions required to have grace restored to us. When someone pleads fervently in prayer for an answer, the answer may be more conditioned on repentance of personal sins than on any other factor. (See D&C 101:7–8; Mosiah 11:23–24) (Gene R. Cook, "Receiving Divine Assistance through the Grace of the Lord," *Ensign*, May 1993, 79)

Don't Procrastinate Your Repentance

But behold, your days of probation are past; ye have procrastinated the day of your salvation until it is everlastingly too late, and your destruction is made sure. (Helaman 13:38)

Such indulgence in premeditated sin shows pitiful misunderstanding of repentance. As Amulek warned, we must not procrastinate the day of our repentance until the end (see Alma 34:32–35). Judgment for us could be today or tomorrow. We must not risk our opportunity to repent. Salvation is not just an escape from the penalty of sin but deliverance from sinfulness. The truly penitent not only seek forgiveness for past sins but plead for the Savior to purge their hearts of the desire or appetite for sin. (J. Richard Clarke, "The Lord of Life," *Ensign*, May 1993, 9)

Jesus Is the Christ

The Lord's duly ordained Apostles . . . declare:

"Jesus is the Living Christ, the immortal Son of God. He is the great King Immanuel, who stands today on the right hand of His Father. He is the light, the life, and the hope of the world. His way is the path that leads to happiness in this life and eternal life in the world to come. God be thanked for the matchless gift of His divine Son."

Jesus, the very thought of Thee fills my heart with *inexpressible joy*. It controls every part of my being.

My life, my loves, my ambitions are molded, enlivened, and given purpose because I know that Thou art the Christ, the Holy One. (Keith B. McMullin, "Jesus, the Very Thought of Thee," *Ensign*, May 2004, 33)

Shun Contention

Through love of God, the pain caused by the fiery canker of contention will be extinguished from the soul. This healing begins with a personal vow: "Let there be peace on earth, and let it begin with me" ("Let There Be Peace on Earth," Sy Miller and Jill Jackson, Jan-Lee Music, Beverly Hills, Calif., 1972). This commitment will then spread to family and friends and will bring peace to neighborhoods and nations.

Shun contention. Seek godliness. Be enlightened by eternal truth. Be like-minded with the Lord in love and united with Him in faith. Then shall the peace of God, which passeth all understanding (Philippians 4:7), be yours, to bless you and your posterity through generations yet to come. (Russell M. Nelson, "The Canker of Contention," *Ensign*, May 1989, 68)

Come unto Christ and Be Perfected in Him

The prophets proclaim, and the scriptures sweetly certify, that all men and women, if they are to achieve true happiness, must come unto Christ and be perfected in Him. To achieve such supernal joy requires a life of dedication and devotion to duty and Deity, a life of service and sacrifice, a life of keeping the commandments. Such a life is characterized by partaking of holy ordinances and by making and keeping sacred covenants, those solemn, celestial agreements between man and God. (Alexander B. Morrison, *Feed My Sheep: Leadership Ideas for Latter-day Shepherds*, [1992], 61)

Blessed Are All They That Mourn

And again, blessed are all they that mourn, for they shall be comforted. (3 Nephi 12:4)

The mourner shall be comforted when he sees the divine purpose in his grief. The Lord has told us: "Come unto me, all ye that labour and are heavy laden, and I will give you rest." (Matthew 11:28) . . .

We must not allow ourselves to become embittered in times of mourning and sorrow. We must keep faith and seek comfort from the Lord through prayer. We have his promise that we shall be blessed. Those who are burdened shall be made happy when they learn the real comfort of the gospel through their faith and *through their works*. (O. Leslie Stone, "The Beatitudes," *Ensign*, Nov. 1974, 31)

Blessed Are the Meek

And blessed are the meek, for they shall inherit the earth. (3 Nephi 12:5)

And what of the meek? In a world too preoccupied with winning through intimidation and seeking to be number one, no large crowd of folk is standing in line to buy books that call for mere meekness. But the meek shall inherit the earth, a pretty impressive corporate takeover—and done *without* intimidation! Sooner or later, and we pray sooner *than* later, everyone will acknowledge that Christ's way is not only the *right* way, but ultimately the *only* way to hope and joy. Every knee shall bow and every tongue will confess that gentleness is better than brutality, that kindness is greater than coercion, that the soft voice turneth away wrath. In the end, and sooner than that whenever possible, we must be more like him. "To those who fall, how kind thou art!/How good to those who seek!" (Howard W. Hunter, "Jesus, the Very Thought of Thee," *Ensign*, May 1993, 63)

Blessed Are All They Who Do Hunger and Thirst after Righteousness

And blessed are all they who do hunger and thirst after righteousness, for they shall be filled with the Holy Ghost. (3 Nephi 12:6)

All around us we have the good examples of those who seek permanent treasures—those who "hunger and thirst after righteousness" (Matthew 5:6) and put the kingdom of God first in their lives. Among the most visible such examples are the men and women who set aside their worldly pursuits and even say good-bye to their families to serve missions for the Lord. Tens of thousands of these are young missionaries. In addition, I pay particular tribute to those who serve missions in their mature years, some as mission leaders and some as what we call couple missionaries. Their remarkable service evidences their priorities, and their impressive example is a guide to their families and to all who know them. (Dallin H. Oaks, "Focus and Priorities," *Ensign*, May 2001, 82)

Blessed Are the Merciful

And blessed are the merciful, for they shall obtain mercy. (3 Nephi 12:7)

How godlike a quality is mercy. It cannot be legislated. It must come from the heart. It must be stirred up from within. It is part of the endowment each of us receives as a son or daughter of God and partaker of a divine birthright. I plead for an effort among all of us to give greater expression and wider latitude to this instinct which lies within us. I am convinced that there comes a time, possibly many times, within our lives when we might cry out for mercy on the part of others. How can we expect it unless we have been merciful ourselves? (Gordon B. Hinckley, "Blessed Are the Merciful," *Ensign*, May 1990, 68)

Blessed Are All the Pure in Heart

And blessed are all the pure in heart, for they shall see God. (3 Nephi 12:8)

When [Christ] spoke of being without guile, he referred to something far deeper than outward appearance. He was reaching into the soul, to the very heart of righteousness. He was touching the key to goodness and to the Christlike life.

To be without guile is to be pure in heart—an essential virtue of those who would be counted among true followers of Christ. . . . He revealed to the Prophet Joseph Smith that Zion is the pure in heart (see D&C 97:21) and that a house is to be built in Zion in which the pure in heart shall see God (see D&C 97:10–16). (Joseph B. Wirthlin, "Without Guile," *Ensign*, May 1988, 80)

Blessed Are All the Peacemakers

And blessed are all the peacemakers, for they shall be called the children of God.
(3 Nephi 12:9)

To err is human, to forgive divine (Alexander Pope, *An Essay on Criticism*, 2:1711). There is no peace in harboring old grudges. There is no peace in reflecting on the pain of old wounds. There is peace only in repentance and forgiveness. This is the sweet peace of the Christ, who said, "Blessed are the peacemakers; for they shall be called the children of God" (Matthew 5:9). (Gordon B. Hinckley,

"Of You It Is Required to Forgive," *Ensign*, Nov. 1980, 61)

Blessed Are All They Who Are Persecuted for My Name's Sake

> And blessed are all they who are persecuted for my name's sake, for theirs is the kingdom of heaven.
> And blessed are ye when men shall revile you and persecute, and shall say all manner of evil against you falsely, for my sake;
> For ye shall have great joy and be exceedingly glad, for great shall be your reward in heaven; for so persecuted they the prophets who were before you. (3 Nephi 12:10–12)

We are to love the Lord, our God, with all our hearts and our neighbors as ourselves. We are even to love our enemies, to bless them that curse us, do good to them that hate us and pray for them which despitefully use us, and persecute us, following the example of Jesus who, when being persecuted to the death, prayed to the Father to forgive his persecutors. This represents the true spirit of Christ which should motivate all our life's actions. (George F. Richards, in Conference Report, Oct. 1947, 55)

Let Your Light Shine

Therefore let your light so shine before this people, that they may see your good works and glorify your Father who is in heaven.
(3 Nephi 12:16)

Those then who are the "salt of the earth" are also the light of the world, and the radiance of that light, shining through their good works to mankind, glorifies our Eternal Father and strengthens his work and kingdom on the earth.

One of the best compliments an individual can say of another is that he or she is the "salt of the earth." It is most meaningful and suggests unquestioned Christlike character and conduct, uprightness, honesty, spirituality, sincerity of purpose, dignity, and other noble character virtues and qualities patterned after the divine nature of our Heavenly Father. (Delbert L. Stapley, in Conference Report, Oct. 1964, 65)

Love Everyone

And behold it is written also, that thou shalt love thy neighbor and hate thine enemy; But behold I say unto you, love your enemies, bless them that curse you, do good to them that hate you, and pray for them who despitefully use you and persecute you. (3 Nephi 12:43–44)

Imagine for a moment the result if everyone were to love one another as Jesus loves his disciples. We would have no bickering, quarreling, strife, or contention in our homes. We would not offend or insult one another either verbally or in any other way. We would not have unnecessary litigation over small matters. War would be impossible, especially war waged in the name of religion. (Joseph B. Wirthlin, "Our Lord and Savior," *Ensign*, Nov. 1993, 5)

Becoming Perfect

Therefore I would that ye should be perfect even as I, or your Father who is in heaven is perfect. (3 Nephi 12:48)

I would emphasize that the teachings of Christ that we should become perfect were not mere rhetoric.

He meant literally that it is the right of mankind to become like the Father and like the Son, having overcome human weaknesses and developed attributes of divinity.

Because many individuals do not fully use the capacity that is in them does nothing to negate the truth that they have the power to become Christlike. It is the man and woman who use the power who prove its existence; neglect cannot prove its absence.

Working toward perfection is not a one-time decision but a process to be pursued throughout one's lifetime. (Spencer W. Kimball, "Hold Fast to the Iron Rod," *Ensign*, Nov. 1978, 4)

Pray with a Pure Heart

The young Joseph Smith showed us how to pray. . . . He believed in the promise he read in the book of James. He went to the grove with faith that his prayer would be answered. He wanted to know which church to join. He was submissive enough to be ready to do whatever he was told to do. So he prayed, as we must, already committed to obey.

What he was told to do required his whole soul and finally his life. He endured during the 24 years that followed by continuing to pray with that childlike faith and humility. We can teach those we love to pray with the intent to obey. We can promise them they will gain the companionship of the Holy Ghost. The Spirit will testify the truth to their hearts every time they read in the scriptures which came to us through the Prophet Joseph Smith. And the Spirit will confirm again that God spoke through His prophet. (Henry B. Eyring, "An Enduring Testimony of the Mission of the Prophet Joseph," *Ensign*, Nov. 2003, 89)

Forgive Men Their Trespasses

For, if ye forgive men their trespasses your heavenly Father will also forgive you;
But if ye forgive not men their trespasses neither will your Father forgive your trespasses.
(3 Nephi 13:14–15)

Closely related to our own obligation to repent is the generosity of letting others do the same—we are to forgive even as we are forgiven. In this we participate in the very essence of the Atonement of Jesus Christ. Surely the most majestic moment of that fateful Friday, when nature convulsed and the veil of the temple was rent, was that unspeakably merciful moment when Christ said, "Father, forgive them; for they know not what they do." As our advocate with the Father, He is still making that same plea today—in your behalf and in mine. (Jeffrey R. Holland, "The Peaceable Things of the Kingdom," *Ensign*, Nov. 1996, 82)

Your Eye Single to the Glory of God

The light of the body is the eye; if, therefore, thine eye be single, thy whole body shall be full of light.
But if thine eye be evil, thy whole body shall be full of darkness. If, therefore, the light that is in thee be darkness, how great is that darkness!
(3 Nephi 13:22–23)

To love God more than anything else impels us to take control of our priorities and order our lives so as to be in accord with Him. We come to love all of God's creations, including our fellowman. Placing God first in all things kindles greater love and devotion between husband and wife, parents and children. In Zion, we find "every man seeking the interest of his neighbor, and doing all things with an eye single to the glory of God." (Keith B. McMullin, "Come to Zion! Come to Zion!" *Ensign*, Nov. 2002, 94)

No Man Can Serve Two Masters

No man can serve two masters; for either he will hate the one and love the other, or else he will hold to the one and despise the other. Ye cannot serve God and Mammon. (3 Nephi 13:24)

The exact opposite of such vacillating is the life and character of the one to whom we should hold fast as the very ideal of integrity—Jesus Christ, the Savior, who taught that man cannot live a divided life, that he cannot serve both God and mammon, and that he cannot serve two masters. Not only were Christ's teachings directed to a oneness of purpose, but his own life was the personification of integrity. This virtue is one of our greatest needs today. (N. Eldon Tanner, "Integrity," *Ensign*, May 1977, 14)

Seek Ye First the Kingdom of God

But seek ye first the kingdom of God and his righteousness, and all these things shall be added unto you. (3 Nephi 13:33)

All can claim that promise. The youngest and the newest member can seek to build up the kingdom of God. Zion is made up of individuals and families. When their faith increases, the kingdom is established more firmly. We can try to help with that every day. Even the smallest act to build faith in another person or in a family qualifies us for the gift and power of the Holy Ghost. The Holy Ghost testifies of truth. Therefore, in our service, our faith increases that Jesus is the Christ, that our Heavenly Father lives and loves us, and that Joseph was Their prophet. You can expect that, every time you go to a home to build faith, as a home teacher or a visiting teacher or a friend. (Henry B. Eyring, "An Enduring Testimony of the Mission of the Prophet Joseph," *Ensign*, Nov. 2003, 89)

The Golden Rule

Therefore, all things whatsoever ye would that men should do to you, do ye even so to them, for this is the law and the prophets. (3 Nephi 14:12)

Wherever it is found and however it is expressed, the Golden Rule encompasses the moral code of the kingdom of God. It forbids interference by one with the rights of another. It is equally binding upon nations, associations, and individuals. With compassion and forbearance, it replaces the retaliatory reactions of "an eye for an eye, and a tooth for a tooth." If we were to stay on that old and unproductive path, we would be but blind and toothless. (Russell M. Nelson, "Blessed Are the Peacemakers," *Ensign*, Nov. 2002, 39)

Wherefore, By Their Fruits Ye Shall Know Them

Wherefore, by their fruits ye shall know them. (3 Nephi 14:20)

The Savior gave the criteria for His friendship in the 15th chapter of John, in which He states, "Ye are my friends, if ye do whatsoever I command you" (John 15:14). He further gave the acid test when He said, "Ye shall know them by their fruits" (Matthew 7:16; see also Matthew 7:17–18, 20). This is how we will all be judged—by our fruits, good or bad. In the final judgment, if our fruits so warrant, we will be invited to sit on the right hand of God. There I believe will be His friends. (Richard C. Edgley, "A Disciple, a Friend," *Ensign*, May 1998, 11)

True Discipleship

True disciples are those who go beyond simply believing. They act out their belief. Said the Savior, "If any man will *do his will, he shall know of the doctrine*, whether it be of God, or whether I speak of myself (John 7:17; italics added). Disciples follow the Divine Master. Their actions speak in symphonic harmony with their beliefs. They know who they are. They know what God expects of them. They mirror inner peace and certainty concerning the mission and resurrection of Christ. They hunger and thirst after righteousness. They know they are here on this earth for a purpose. They understand life after death. They believe that the transcendent event in the ministry of the Christ was the Atonement, culminating in the Resurrection. (James E. Faust, "The Resurrection," *Ensign*, May 1985, 30)

Teach with Exhortation

Nephi taught his brothers: "Whoso would hearken unto the word of God, and would hold fast unto it, they would never perish; neither could the temptations and the fiery darts of the adversary overpower them unto blindness, to lead them away to destruction" (1 Nephi 15:24).

Then he gave this example of how to teach: "I did exhort them with all the energies of my soul, and with all the faculty which I possessed, that they would give heed to the word of God and remember to keep his commandments always in all things." (1 Nephi 15:25) (Richard G. Scott, "To Help a Loved One in Need," *Ensign*, May 1988, 60)

Live What You Teach

Behold, I have given unto you the commandments; therefore keep my commandments. And this is the law and the prophets, for they truly testified of me. (3 Nephi 15:10)

Let us try to live our religion, and try to be friends of God; and let us make war against the works of the devil. Let us seek to overcome ourselves, and all our evil impressions, and bring our bodies in subjection to the law of Christ, that we may walk in the light of the Lord, gain power with him, and assist in sanctifying the earth and in building up temples, and in attending to the ordinances of the house of

God, that we may be saviors of men, both of the living and the dead. These are our privileges, and the blessings which the God of heaven has put into our hands. (Heber J. Grant, in Conference Report, Apr. 1933, 12)

Our Sacrifice

When we are urged to put upon the altar of the Lord the sacrifice of a broken heart and a contrite spirit (Psalm 51:17; 3 Nephi 9:20), we are following the ancient counsel: "to obey is better than sacrifice, and to hearken than the fat of rams" (1 Sam. 15:22). Outward rituals can become near-empty ends in themselves. What we are actually placing on the altar to be consumed is the animal and carnal of our old selves. The need for that sacrifice has not been done away.

Spiritual submissiveness is not blind faith but deliberate obedience. (Neal A. Maxwell, *Not My Will, But Thine* [1998], 99–100)

Where Is Your Heart?

Behold, the Lord requireth the heart and a willing mind; and the willing and obedient shall eat the good of the land of Zion in these last days. (D&C 64:34)

When the Lord measures an individual. . . . He measures the heart as an indicator of the person's capacity and potential to bless others.

Why the heart? Because the heart is a symbol of one's entire makeup. . . .

The measure of our hearts is the measure of our total performance. As the term is used by the Lord, our hearts describe our efforts to better ourselves or others or the conditions we confront. (Marvin J. Ashton, *The Measure of Our Hearts* [1991], 2)

Testify with Power

In order to testify, one's mind has to function, and it must be concentrated upon the thing to be testified. And we are not only to partake of the emblems of the sacrament in remembrance of the Redeemer, testifying that we do always remember him, but we are also thereby to witness unto the Father that we are willing to take upon us the name of his Son and that we will keep his commandments. This amounts to a virtual renewal of the covenant of baptism, for you will recall that candidates for baptism are, among other things, to . . . witness before the church that they . . . are willing to take upon them the name of Jesus Christ, having a determination to serve him to the end. (D&C 20:37) (Marion G. Romney, in Conference Report, Apr. 1946, 40)

Watch and Pray Always

Behold, verily, verily, I say unto you, ye must watch and pray always lest ye enter into temptation; for Satan desireth to have you, that he may sift you as wheat. (3 Nephi 18:18)

Prayer is one of the greatest blessings we have while here on earth. Through prayer we can communicate with our Heavenly Father and seek His guidance daily. Jesus taught, "Ye must always pray unto the Father in my name" (3 Nephi 18:19). We should pray each day that we will have the power to resist temptation. Amulek teaches us that we should pray "morning, mid-day, and evening" and that our hearts should "be full, drawn out in prayer unto [God] continually" (Alma 34:21, 27). Our daily prayers influence our thoughts, our words, and our actions. In order to retain a remission of our sins, it is essential that we ask our Heavenly Father each day for strength to stay in the straight and narrow way. (Keith Crockett, "Retaining a Remission of Sin," *Ensign*, Nov. 2000, 77)

Purified through Christ the Lord

Father, I thank thee that thou hast purified those whom I have chosen, because of their faith, and I pray for them, and also for them who shall believe on their words, that they may be purified in me, through faith on their words, even as they are purified in me. (3 Nephi 19:28)

That is what it means in Moroni when it says, "Relying alone upon the merits of Christ, who was the author and the finisher of their faith" (Moroni 6:4). It is the Savior who made possible our being purified through His Atonement and our obedience to His commandments. And it is the Savior who will nourish those who go down in faith into the waters of baptism and receive the gift of the Holy Ghost. When they always remember Him, and when they continue in childlike obedience, it is He who will assure that they have His Spirit always to be with them. (Henry B. Eyring, "Feed My Lambs," *Ensign*, Nov. 1997, 82)

Go with a Prayer in Your Heart

And it came to pass that he commanded the multitude that they should cease to pray, and also his disciples. And he commanded them that they should not cease to pray in their hearts. (3 Nephi 20:1)

That is taught clearly in Alma in the Book of Mormon:

"Yea, and when you do not cry unto the Lord, let your hearts be full, drawn out in prayer unto him continually for your welfare, and also for the welfare of those who are around you."Our hearts can only be drawn out to God when they are filled with love for Him and trust in His goodness. Joseph Smith, even as a boy, gave us an example of how we can come to pray from a heart filled with the love of God and then pray unceasingly through a life filled with trials and blessings. (Henry B. Eyring, "Prayer," *Ensign*, Nov. 2001, 15)

President Monson's Testimony of You

Serving throughout the world is a great missionary force, going about doing good as did the Savior.

Missionaries teach truth. They dispel darkness. They spread joy. They bring precious souls to Christ. . . .

The full-time missionaries and all others engaged in the work of the Lord have answered His call. We are on His errand. We shall succeed in the solemn charge given by Mormon to declare the Lord's word among the people. Wrote Mormon: "Behold, I am a disciple of Jesus Christ, the Son of God. I have been called of him to declare his word among his people, that they might have everlasting life." (Thomas S. Monson, "Today Determines Tomorrow," *Ensign*, Nov. 1998, 48)

The Power of the Love of God

Responding to true love is part of our very being. We innately desire to reconnect here with the love we felt there. Only as we feel God's love and fill our hearts with His love can we be truly happy.

God's love fills the immensity of space; therefore, there is no shortage of love in the universe, only in our willingness to do what is needed to feel it. To do this, Jesus explained we must "love the Lord thy God with all thy heart, soul, strength, and mind; and thy neighbour as thyself" (Luke 10:27).

The more we obey God, the more we desire to help others. The more we help others, the more we love God and on and on. Conversely, the more we disobey God and the more selfish we are, the less love we feel. (John H. Groberg, "The Power of God's Love," *Ensign*, Nov. 2004, 9)

Love Begets Love

The Prophet Joseph Smith tells us that love begets love in this way: "It is a time-honored adage that love begets love. Let us pour forth love—show forth our kindness unto all mankind, and the Lord will reward us with everlasting increase; cast our bread upon the waters and we shall receive it after many days, increased to a hundredfold."

This most important part of the gospel is the very foundation of God's commandments, for he said: "Thou shalt love the Lord thy God with all thy heart, with all thy might, mind, and strength; and in the name of Jesus Christ thou shalt serve him. (Adney Y. Komatsu, "Faith and Works in the Far East," *Ensign*, Nov. 1975, 88)

My Mission

And I would that I could persuade all ye ends of the earth to repent and prepare to stand before the judgment-seat of Christ. (Mormon 3:22)

Our mission is to preach "Jesus Christ, and him crucified" (1 Corinthians 2:2). Our mission is to proclaim the message of reconciliation to all men. Our mission also is to persuade men to forsake their sins, to "come unto Christ, and be perfected in him," and to deny themselves "of all ungodliness." (Moroni 10:32)

"How great the importance to make these things known unto the inhabitants of the earth, that they may know that there is no flesh that can dwell in the presence of God, save it be through the merits, and mercy, and grace of the Holy Messiah," and then only when they believe and obey his laws. (2 Nephi 2:8) (Bruce R. McConkie, *The Promised Messiah: The First Coming of Christ* [1978], 262)

Why Do People Fall Away?

The Doctrine and Covenants tells us that the Book of Mormon is the "record of a fallen people"

(D&C 20:9). Why did they fall? This is one of the major messages of the Book of Mormon. Mormon gives the answer in the closing chapters of the book in these words: "Behold, the pride of this nation, or the people of the Nephites, hath proven their destruction" (Moroni 8:27). And then, lest we miss that momentous Book of Mormon message from that fallen people, the Lord warns us in the Doctrine and Covenants, "Beware of pride, lest ye become as the Nephites of old." (D&C 38:39) (Ezra Taft Benson, "Beware of Pride," *Ensign*, May 1989, 4)

The Lifeline of Prayer

When God placed man on the earth, prayer became the lifeline between mankind and God. Thus, in Adam's generation, men began "to call upon the name of the Lord." Through all generations since that time, prayer has filled a very important human need. Each of us has problems that we cannot solve and weaknesses that we cannot conquer without reaching out through prayer to a higher source of strength. That source is the God of heaven to whom we pray in the name of Jesus

Christ. As we pray we should think of our Father in Heaven as possessing all knowledge, understanding, love, and compassion. (James E. Faust, "The Lifeline of Prayer," *Ensign*, May 2002, 59)

Exercising Faith

Motivating faith is centered in trust in the Lord and in His willingness to answer your needs. For "the Lord . . . doth bless and prosper those who put their trust in him." The consistent, willing exercise of faith increases your confidence and ability to employ the power of faith. You can learn to use faith more. . . .

He will prompt you to do that which will increase your ability to act in faith. With consistent practice, faith will become a vibrant, powerful, uplifting, inspiring force in your life. As you walk to the boundary of your understanding into the twilight of uncertainty, exercising faith, you will be led to find solutions you would not obtain otherwise. I testify that I know that is true. (Richard G. Scott, "The Sustaining Power of Faith in Times of Uncertainty and Testing," *Ensign*, May 2003, 75)

Gaining Hope

Wherefore, ye may also have hope, and be partakers of the gift, if ye will but have faith. (Ether 12:9)

That kind of redeeming faith, Mormon taught, leads to hope, a special, theological kind of hope. The word is often used to express the most general of aspirations—wishes, if you will. But as used in the Book of Mormon it is very specific and flows naturally from one's faith in Christ. "How is it that ye can attain unto faith, save ye shall [as a consequence] have hope?" Mormon asked. This is the same faith-leads-to-hope sequence that Moroni used, saying, "Ye may also have hope . . . if ye will but have faith." (Jeffrey R. Holland, *Christ and the New Covenant: The Messianic Message of the Book of Mormon* [1997], 334)

Growth through Adversity

The revelations, for which we are grateful, show that we should even give thanks for our afflictions because they turn our hearts to God and give us opportunities to prepare for what God would have us become. The Lord taught the prophet Moroni, "I give unto men weakness that they may be humble," and then promised that "if they humble themselves and have faith in me, then will I make weak things become strong unto them" (Ether 12:27). In the midst of the persecutions the Latter-day Saints were suffering in Missouri, the Lord gave a similar teaching and promise: "Verily I say unto you my friends, fear not, let your hearts be comforted; yea, rejoice evermore, and in everything give thanks; and all things wherewith you have been afflicted shall work together for your good. (D&C 98:1, 3) (Dallin H. Oaks, "Give Thanks in All Things," *Ensign*, May 2003, 95)

Making the Sacrament More Meaningful

I learned that as we sing the sacrament hymns with real intent, phrases like "How great the wisdom and the love" or "Dearly, dearly has he loved! And we must love him too" will swell our hearts with love and gratitude (see "How Great the Wisdom and the Love," *Hymns*, no. 195; "There Is a Green Hill Far Away," *Hymns*, no. 194). As we sincerely listen to the sacrament prayers, phrases such as "always remember him," "keep his commandments," "have his Spirit to be with them" will fill our hearts with an overwhelming desire to be better (see D&C 20:77, 79). Then when we partake of the bread and the water with a broken heart and a contrite spirit, I know we can feel and even hear those most wondrous words "I love you. I love you." (John H. Groberg, "The Power of God's Love," *Ensign*, Nov. 2004, 9)

Make Changes and Repent

But as oft as they repented and sought forgiveness, with real intent, they were forgiven. (Moroni 6:8)

Many of you are already on this track, and we commend you for your worthiness and determination. For those of you who are not, let tonight be the beginning of your preparation process. If you find yourself wanting in worthiness, resolve to make the appropriate changes—beginning right now. If you think you need to talk to your father and your bishop about any sins you may have committed, don't wait; do it now. They will help you to repent and change so you can take your place as a member of the greatest generation of missionaries. (M. Russell Ballard, "The Greatest Generation of Missionaries," *Ensign*, Nov. 2002, 46)

Missionaries Are the Peaceable Followers of Christ

Missionaries return home with a love for the people they have served and taught. They are true ambassadors spreading goodwill for the peoples in whose countries they have lived and worked. They are not concerned with income levels and have no racial bias. They are not out to build any worldly kingdoms. They are, in the words of Mormon, "the peaceable followers of Christ" (Moroni 7:3). The only kingdom which interests them is the kingdom of our Lord and Savior which He will establish at His return. Their only hope is to prepare us for that great day. (L. Tom Perry, "The Peaceable Followers of Christ," *Ensign*, Nov. 1989, 70)

Getting Along with Missionary Companions Teaches Unselfishness

I find some difficulty between missionaries. Brothers and sisters, that's one of the tests for which you are here on the proving ground. If you can't get along with your companion, how can you get along with the person you choose to live with for the rest of your life? For your own sake, you must fit into your companion's life and adjust. Perhaps your homes are different. Grit your teeth and say, "I am going to give about 90 percent and I will only take 10 percent." You have to "give and take" in every phase of life. How are you going to get along with a wife or husband? Just exactly the same way, a life of unselfishness and consideration for others. You must think of the other, love him more than your own self, and then you will have success. Marriage is not something which when you press a button you get happiness. You have to make happiness in marriage the same as in the mission field. Instead of fighting for your own pleasure, you are fighting for the pleasure of the other. (Spencer W. Kimball, *The Teachings of Spencer W. Kimball*, ed. Edward L. Kimball [1982], 579)

Love Is the Purification of the Heart

For behold, God hath said a man being evil cannot do that which is good; for if he offereth a gift, or prayeth unto God, except he shall do it with real intent it profiteth him nothing.
(Moroni 7:6)

Love is the purification of the heart. It strengthens character and gives a higher motive and a positive aim to every action of life. The power to love truly and devotedly is the noblest gift with which a human being can be endowed. True love is eternal and infinite. It is equal and pure without violent actions and demonstrations which are so much in evidence today. (Delbert L. Stapley, in Conference Report, Oct. 1970, 45)

The Holy Spirit Will Lead Us to Do Good

We take the sacrament in remembrance of the suffering of our Lord and covenant to keep his commandments that we may always have his Spirit to be with us. His Spirit will not lead us to do anything that is evil but will encourage us to do good, and by following that persuasion and by maintaining that guidance, we will grow in nearness to the Lord; we will grow in good deeds; and we will overcome the flesh. A man who has the companionship of the Spirit of the Lord is a happy man. He can be a thoughtful and faithful patriarch and leader in his home and family; he is a good neighbor; he can be an influence for good among his neighbors. (Joseph

Anderson, "Being Anxiously Engaged," *Ensign*, May 1978, 68)

True Conversion

Stated simply, true conversion is the fruit of *faith*, *repentance*, and *consistent obedience*. *Faith* comes by hearing the word of God and responding to it. You will receive from the Holy Ghost a confirming witness of things you accept on *faith* by willingly doing them. You will be led to *repent* of errors resulting from wrong things done or right things not done. As a consequence, your capacity to *consistently obey* will be strengthened. This cycle of *faith*, *repentance*, and *consistent obedience* will lead you to greater conversion with its attendant blessings. True conversion will strengthen your capacity to do what you know you should do, when you should do it, regardless of the circumstances. (Richard G. Scott, "Full Conversion Brings Happiness," *Ensign*, May 2002, 24)

Missionaries—Don't Return and Settle Back into Old Ways

Now the time's going to come when your missions will be terminated and you will be given an honorable release. As soon as you come out of the mission field, a new life ahead, it's going to be a change. You won't feel at ease at first, coming back into civilian life, because it's going to be different, different than what you had expected. There's going to be a question as to whether you are going to come home and fall in with the rest, or whether you're going to keep the enthusiasm for missionary work that you have today. Oh, I'd be disappointed in any elder here who came home and settled back into old ways. (Howard W. Hunter, *The Teachings of Howard W. Hunter* [1997], 254)

Living in Thanksgiving Daily

Truly, it is fitting to give thanks to the Lord, and to talk of all His wondrous work; and in doing so, we must include the greatest of all of His blessings—the sending of His Only Begotten Son, to give to all our Father's children redemption, and to those who will listen and obey the Gospel, salvation and exaltation in the kingdom of our Father. Obedience to the principles of the Gospel brings happiness, and happiness is what all men seek. (David O. McKay, *Pathways to Happiness* [1957], 104)

Remember Your Discipleship

"Behold, I am a disciple of Jesus Christ, the Son of God. I have been called of him to declare his word among his people, that they might have everlasting life." (3 Nephi 5:13)

"A new commandment I give unto you, That ye love one another; as I have loved you, that ye also love one another. By this shall all men know that ye are my disciples, if ye have love one to another." (John 13:34–35)

"Therefore let your light so shine before this people, that they may see your good works and glorify your Father who is in heaven." (3 Nephi 12:16)

"He that receiveth my law and doeth it, the same is my disciple; and he that saith he receiveth it and doeth it not, the same is not my disciple, and shall be cast out from among you." (D&C 41:5)

Devoted followers of the Lord Jesus Christ are true disciples. The sacrifice is great; the reward is eternal life. We live His doctrine and precepts. We preach and teach His word and His gospel. We all can be His true disciples. There is no comparison by title, position, or station; there is no competition with others. There is only one question: Do we do the will of God?

About the Author

Ed J. Pinegar is the author of more than sixty nonfiction books, audio books, and talks.

He has had the opportunity to teach at Brigham Young University, the Orem Institute of Religion, the Provo MTC, various seminaries, and BYU Education Week. He has been blessed with the opportunity to serve in many positions of leadership within The Church of Jesus Christ of Latter-day Saints, most recently serving as the Manti Temple president.

He and his wife, Pat, are the parents of eight, grandparents of thirty-eight, and great-grandparents of twenty-five. Ed and his wife live in Orem, Utah.